A Faithful FUTURE

Teaching and Learning for Discipleship

Contributors: Carol F. Krau
Judith M. Bunyi
N. Lynne Westfield
Joyce Brown
Barbara Bruce
Ben Marshall

DISCIPLESHIP RESOURCES

P.O. BOX 340003 • NASHVILLE, TN 37203-0003
www.discipleshipresources.org

Cover and book design by Sharon Anderson

ISBN 0-88177-281-X

Library of Congress Catalog Card No. 98-61198

DR281

Contents

Introduction

If you are looking at this resource, you are probably one of the leaders in your congregation with responsibility for identifying and equipping Sunday school teachers and other small-group leaders. I know from experience that it is an awesome and somewhat overwhelming task. It is also one of the most significant responsibilities in a congregation.

A part of our responsibility is to clearly articulate what it is that we hope to accomplish through our small-group ministries. In a phrase, it is to make disciples for Jesus Christ. Centuries ago, the apostle Paul spoke of this responsibility in his letter to the church in Ephesus. With deep passion and eloquence he wrote:

> There is one body and one Spirit, just as you were called to the one hope of your calling, one Lord, one faith, one baptism, one God and Father of all, who is above all and through all and in all. But each of us was given grace according to the measure of Christ's gift...to equip the saints for the work of ministry, for building up the body of Christ, until all of us come to the unity of the faith and of the knowledge of the Son of God, to maturity, to the measure of the full stature of Christ.
>
> (Ephesians 4:4-7, 12-13)

Equipping the saints—that's what we're about! This biblical passage reminds us of the deeply spiritual work teachers and leaders have to do in their classes and small groups. Together as we pray, study the Scriptures, worship, and support one another in growing in faith, we build communities that are centered in Christ, that are open to God's Spirit, that are growing toward maturity, and that are seeking to live as disciples of Jesus Christ in every arena of life.

Sunday school classes, youth groups, and other small groups are vital in supporting children, youth, and adults as they seek to live in relationship with God and one another through the power of the Holy Spirit. The give-and-take of theological reflection, Bible study, prayer, outreach, worship, and advocacy challenges us to deepen and broaden our understanding of what Jesus calls us to do and be in the world today, both as individuals and as communities.

Leadership for small-group ministries is a key component to the success of such an endeavor. The spiritual leadership needed for teaching and leading small groups is of major concern in many congregations. The context in which the church operates and which the church hopes to address has changed drastically in the last half-century. There are a variety of factors impacting leadership in our churches. Among them are the following:

- It is common for families and individuals to move several times over the course of time. Therefore, congregational leadership is transitory, and it is difficult to build a core group of experienced leadership within a congregation.
- Adults today do not participate in a particular congregation out of a sense of denominational loyalty. Many members in United Methodist congregations come from a variety of denominational backgrounds. They are unequipped, and possibly unmotivated, to teach from a Wesleyan perspective.
- Many adults under the age of fifty, who are frequently asked to serve as teachers, are unfamiliar with much of the Bible.

Equipping the saints—that's what we're about!

5

- Sundays and Wednesdays are no longer protected times for learning and growing in faith, and no other day or time has taken precedence. Our congregations' members have multiple demands on them, and we cannot assume that they will choose the church as their first priority.
- Women, who were once the majority of the church's volunteers, increasingly work outside the home. Therefore, they are no longer able to give as much time to their congregations.
- Our fast-food mentality is in tension with the in-depth demands of Christian discipleship. We sometimes feel uncertain about committing the time and energy needed to practice the spiritual disciplines and prepare for leading a group.

Sounds like bad news, doesn't it? I'm really not trying to depress you. I just think it's crucial to be realistic about what's going on in our world and in our congregations. Unless we know where we are, it will be difficult—if not impossible—to move to where we want to be.

There is also plenty of good news, too. First, there is documented evidence of a great spiritual yearning and openness in the hearts of people. The evidence comes from church sources as well as from civic sources, such as Gallup Polls, *Time Magazine,* and CNN news. That means we have tremendous opportunities to help people experience God's presence in their lives and learn to live as Christian disciples.

Second, we have enormously expanded our ability to be in touch with people. Television, videos, fax machines, and the Internet provide almost unlimited access to and between people. Direct communication is not only more accessible but also more attractive and inviting. And technology has the capacity to connect us to our global community, as well as to those within our local neighborhoods.

Third, there is a great deal of knowledge about learning styles, personality types, gender issues, interpersonal communication, group dynamics, and so forth. We can draw from this vast storehouse of information as we plan our educational ministries.

Finally, this is a task that we do not fulfill alone. We are called by God to this ministry, and God promises to be with us as we answer the call. As is said in many African American congregations: God is good! All the time! We can count on God's goodness and grace to guide and sustain us. That is truly good news!

How to Use This Resource

In early 1999, Discipleship Resources published *Keeping in Touch: Christian Formation and Teaching.* That resource explores the current context for teaching and learning and proposes the following five critical processes for effective leadership in small groups:

- Keeping in touch with God (strengthening our skills for and commitment to practicing spiritual disciplines);
- Keeping in touch with God's people (listening to and caring for group members);
- Keeping in touch with your experience (developing and improving skills for theological reflection);
- Keeping in touch with the world (participating in the ongoing ministry of the church);

Unless we know where we are, it will be difficult— if not impossible— to move to where we want to be.

■ Keeping in touch with teaching (developing and improving our teaching skills, so that we stay focused on our central task of making disciples for Jesus Christ).

Keeping in Touch is primarily designed to provoke thought and foster dialogue in order to focus on the mission of the church, particularly as it is lived out through small-group settings. It is also intended to provide assistance to congregational leaders in building a conceptual framework for developing capable and faithful small-group leadership that will be sufficient for today's context.

This book, which is a companion piece to *Keeping in Touch,* moves theory into practice. It consists of six sections, one dealing with developing a plan and five dealing with each of the processes identified above. Each section begins with an introductory article for you, the person responsible for planning and implementing ministries of Christian formation in your congregation. Each section also includes a workshop model to use with teachers, reproducible pages to use in the workshop or with individual teachers, and a short list of helpful resources.

You will probably not want or need to begin with Section 1 and work your way through to the end of this book. The sections are not intended to be used sequentially and are not included in order of priority. However, we do suggest that you begin with information from Section 1. After that you will want to pick and choose how you wish to use the material found here. Your congregation is unique. It is in a particular community, where there are particular opportunities and challenges. Your congregation includes people with particular gifts. You and your teachers and small-group leaders will have to determine the priority of needs represented in your congregation.

As you plan, remember that the demands on people's time impact their ability to attend every meeting every time. In the past, we could schedule a meeting and expect people to attend. But those days are long gone—even if we continue to behave as if they are not. Plan to offer a workshop multiple times throughout the year and at different times on different days.

Since each teacher is different, don't expect all teachers to need to build the same knowledge and skills. While you will certainly offer learning opportunities that may appeal to a large number of teachers, you may need to plan specific events for as few as one or two teachers.

You may also wish to cooperate with another congregation in your area. You can pool your resources (material and human) to meet the needs of a larger constituency through this kind of cooperation. When people experience the free flow of ideas and conversation in such groups, they often discover a powerful synergy that fuels clarity of focus and direction.

The gospel of Jesus Christ has the power to transform the world. Teachers and small-group leaders provide opportunities for people of all ages to experience God's transforming presence. It is my hope and my belief that this book will help your congregation on its way to becoming a learning congregation that is intentional and effective in making disciples for Jesus Christ.

Carol F. Krau
Director, Teacher/Leader Development
General Board of Discipleship
The United Methodist Church

Developing a Plan

FOR THE **LEADER**

First things first. Keep the main thing the main thing. Phrases such as these seem to be popping up all over the place these days. Businesses, schools, hospitals, restaurants, and churches are refocusing on the heart of what they do in order to respond more effectively to the people they serve.

Words that were once traditionally limited to churches, such as *mission* and *vision*, appear on signs in places as dissimilar as automobile service departments and fast-food restaurants. A few years ago I attended a conference for the local chapter of the National Middle School Association. One of the plenary speakers declared to the participants: "You did not choose to be a middle school teacher. You were called to be a middle school teacher!" Wow! I was ready to sign up on the spot to teach seventh graders.

What is all this talk about? I believe that in North-American culture, with literally thousands of products and services available to consumers, conversations about mission and vision are essential to clarify what the central core, the essence, of an organization (business, church, and so forth) really is. In The United Methodist Church, we sometimes talk about the primary task of the congregation. The primary task, or mission, is a way of stating what we do that sets us apart from other organizations and makes us unique. It points to what we have to offer that people cannot find anywhere else. It describes what it is that we must do in order to be who we say we are.

As Christians, we understand our primary task as an extension of the life and ministry of Jesus Christ. The Scripture that is most frequently quoted in order to understand our mission is Matthew 28:19-20:

> Go therefore and make disciples of all nations, baptizing them in the name of the Father and of the Son and of the Holy Spirit, and teaching them to obey everything that I have commanded you. And remember, I am with you always, to the end of the age.

by Carol F. Krau

Section 1

When you read these verses, what do they say to you about the primary task of the church? What is it that the church must do in order to be the church and not a school or civic organization? Take a look at the verbs: Go...make (disciples)...baptize...teach...obey...remember. These verbs are clues to the essential identity of the church.

The church is a community of faith centered in Jesus Christ to support the formation of Christian disciples. As the church, we gather to worship God, study the Scriptures, practice spiritual disciplines, enjoy Christian fellowship, and serve the needs of God's people throughout the world. We know from experience that our life together is not a linear process, with a series of steps to be followed. Rather, we engage in an ongoing, multifaceted process of learning what it means to be the people of God.

The following is one way of describing the primary task, which is based on page 115 in *The Book of Discipline of The United Methodist Church–1996.* (See page 15 in this book for a graphic representation of this process.)

We make disciples as we
- Seek and welcome people into the body of Christ;
- Lead people to commit their lives to God through Jesus Christ;
- Nurture people in Christian living;
- Equip and send people to live lovingly and justly as servants of Christ in the world.

This purpose statement of Christian education is another way of describing the primary task:

Through Christian education we invite people and communities of faith to be transformed as they are inspired and challenged to
- Know and experience God through Jesus Christ,
- Claim and live God's promises,
- Grow and serve as Christian disciples.
  (From *Foundations: Shaping the Ministry of Christian Education in Your Congregation,* page 5. © 1993 Discipleship Resources. Used by permission.)

Surprised? The purpose of Christian education is the primary task of the congregation. It is not a part of the primary task. It is the primary task—the whole primary task. The purpose of Christian education is not to teach the Bible. Teaching and studying the Bible is a means to helping people experience God's grace. The purpose of Christian education is not to create morally upright citizens. Living in ways that respect and nurture all people is an obedient, faithful response to God's grace.

The purpose of Christian education is to welcome one another in the name of Jesus Christ, to experience together the transforming power of God's presence, and to discover ways to respond to God's invitation to be God's people in the world. Our teachers and small-group leaders need to be inviting children, youth, and adults to be a part of our Christian community, and they need to welcome them when they participate. As we study, pray, and worship together in our classes, we need to be led into a deeper commitment to live as Christ's disciples. And we need to be equipped for ministry in daily life.

In the past, I have heard teachers say, "I didn't get to the closing worship in the curriculum because I wasn't finished with the lesson." Worshipful

The church is a community of faith centered in Jesus Christ to support the formation of Christian disciples.

study—the closing worship, the opening worship, the in-the-middle worship—is the lesson, just as the biblical material is the lesson. I have noticed how easy it is to be satisfied with whoever attends Sunday school or Bible study. Classes may have long lists of potential class members, based on families who are affiliated with the congregation; yet only a small percentage of those potential members participate. Teachers and other education leaders rarely contact those missing people to encourage them to come. We must develop an invitational style that intentionally seeks and welcomes participation.

We are content to have people show up in the church building for a church activity. We maintain an in-house focus and fail to make the connections between what we do together in the church building and what we do when we are apart in our various homes, neighborhoods, workplaces, and schools. Our small groups must serve as launching pads for equipping people to live as Christians in the world. We are called to serve the world in the name of Jesus.

Our mission, our primary task, is the big picture of who we are and what we do. As teachers and leaders, we need to keep our eye on the big picture. The workshop and tools in this section are designed to help you do that. The remaining sections in this book look at the big picture in a variety of ways to help provide the necessary details for implementing the big picture. As we engage in study, reflection, assessment, and prayer, may we discern God's guidance in how we are living out the primary task of the congregation: making disciples for Jesus Christ.

Helpful Resources

Educating Congregations: The Future of Christian Education, by Charles R. Foster (Nashville: Abingdon Press, 1994).

Educating for Life: A Spiritual Vision for Every Teacher and Parent, by Thomas Groome (Allen, TX: Thomas More Press, 1998).

Foundations: Shaping the Ministry of Christian Education in Your Congregation (Nashville: Discipleship Resources, 1993).

Keeping in Touch: Christian Formation and Teaching, by Carol F. Krau (Nashville: Discipleship Resources, 1999).

Mapping Christian Education: Approaches to Congregational Learning, edited by Jack L. Seymour (Nashville: Abingdon Press, 1997).

Planning for Christian Education: A Practical Guide for Your Congregation, edited by Carol Fouts Krau (Nashville: Discipleship Resources, 1994).

Quest: A Journey Toward a New Kind of Church, by Dan R. Dick, with Evelyn M. Burry (Nashville: Discipleship Resources, 1999).

Sharing Faith: A Comprehensive Approach to Religious Education and Pastoral Ministry, by Thomas H. Groome (San Francisco: Harper SanFrancisco, 1991).

The Learning Congregation: A New Vision of Leadership, by Thomas R. Hawkins (Louisville: Westminster John Knox Press, 1997).

Teacher Development Workshop:
The Primary Task of the Congregation

Purpose

The purpose of this workshop is to help teachers and small-group leaders understand the primary task of the congregation and to explore the ways in which Christian education supports and embodies that task.

Scripture

Luke 10:1-12, 17-20

Time

This session is designed to last approximately one and a half hours.

Materials

- Hymnals
- Photocopies (one per person) of the following:
  "The Primary Task of the Congregation" (page 15)
  "The Purpose of Christian Education" (page 16)
  "Biblical Reflection (Luke 10:1-12, 17-20)" (page 17)
  "Instructions for Bible Study" (page 18)
  "Teaching and the Primary Task Reflection Sheet" (pages 19–20)
  "Building a Learning Plan" (pages 21–22)
- Newsprint
- Felt-tip markers
- Masking tape
- Note cards
- Pencils
- Nametags (optional)

Preparation

- Review the workshop plan and adapt it, as necessary, to your congregation.
- Write the purpose statement of this workshop on newsprint.
- Photocopy the handouts (pages 15–22).
- Gather the supplies listed above.

Workshop Outline

- Gathering and Group Building (10 minutes)
- Workshop Introduction and Beginning Activity (15 minutes)
- Bible Study and Group Reflection (40 minutes)
- Teacher Self-Reflection and Building a Learning Plan (20 minutes)
- Closing (5 minutes)

Workshop Plan

Gathering and Group Building (10 minutes)

❶ Have participants make nametags, if necessary.

❷ Ask participants to find a partner and to stand while they talk briefly about a good book they have read or a good movie they have seen recently. The pairs may sit when they have finished talking (about two minutes per person).

❸ Ask participants to find a new partner and to stand while they name a favorite hymn or Bible story and briefly tell why they like it. The pairs may sit when they have finished talking (about two minutes per person).

❹ When everyone is seated, sing the first stanza of "Go, Make of All Disciples" (*The United Methodist Hymnal*, 571).

Workshop Introduction and Beginning Activity (15 minutes)

❶ Review with the participants the purpose of the workshop (written on newsprint).

❷ On a sheet of newsprint write the word *hospital*. Invite participants to suggest words or phrases that come to mind when they think of a hospital. List their responses on newsprint. After about one minute, ask the group to review their responses. Ask: "What is the one thing that a hospital must do or it wouldn't be a hospital?" Write the response at the bottom of the newsprint. Explain that this essential work of a hospital is the primary task of a hospital.

❸ Repeat the above process using the word *school*. Write the primary task of a school, as identified by the group, at the bottom of the newsprint.

❹ Repeat the above process using the word *church*. Ask group members to identify the primary task of the church. Their responses may include faith formation, discipleship, and being Christian. At the bottom of the newsprint, write "Christian faith and discipleship" as the primary task.

❺ Distribute photocopies of "The Primary Task of the Congregation" (page 15). Using the information from the background article in this section (pages 9–11), talk about the primary task of the church.

❻ Distribute photocopies of "The Purpose of Christian Education" (page 16). Briefly discuss how this purpose relates to and supports the primary task of the church. Point out that our task is more than teaching content or planning lessons; our task is relational and formational.

Bible Study and Group Reflection (40 minutes)

❶ Distribute photocopies of "Biblical Reflection (Luke 10:1-12, 17-20)" (page 17) and "Instructions for Bible Study" (page 18).

❷ Divide the group into smaller groups by having the participants count off A, B, C, and D. Explain that the letter of their small group corresponds with a particular method of Bible study listed on the handout.

③ Allow the small groups to spend approximately twenty-five minutes reading and studying the Scripture, following the instructions on the handout.

④ Ask a person from each small group to report to the total group the highlights of their study and discussion.

Teacher Self-Reflection and Building a Learning Plan (20 minutes)

① Ask the group to stand and sing the second and third stanzas of "Go, Make of All Disciples" (*The United Methodist Hymnal*, 571).

② Distribute photocopies of "Teaching and the Primary Task Reflection Sheet" (pages 19–20) and "Building a Learning Plan" (pages 21–22). Let the participants know that you will be using the information to devise a plan for ongoing learning and skill-building. Give participants about fifteen minutes to complete the forms.

③ Provide each participant with a note card. Ask them to list on the note card their top three priorities from "Building a Learning Plan" and to give the card to you. Their top priority should receive three points. Their second priority should receive two points. Their third priority should receive one point. After the meeting, write on a sheet or newsprint or paper each topic that was listed as a priority. Count the number of points each topic received, and write the total beside each project. (If two people listed "Storytelling" as 3 points, five people listed it as 2, and three people listed it as 1, then the total score for "Storytelling" would be 19—(2x3) + (5x2) + (3x1)=19.

The top-scoring topics are high priorities for your group members. Those topics can become the starting point for your plan for study, practice, and reflection over the next several months. To implement your plan for study, you will need to determine how long each study will be, review resources related to the topic, and identify and secure leadership. To implement a plan for mission/outreach, you will need to identify sites for outreach, determine dates when volunteers are available, plan for orientation and group reflection related to the service, and arrange with the site for your leaders' participation.

Remember that not everyone can participate at the same time. You may want to provide several opportunities throughout the year to attend the same teacher development training. You will also find that teacher-development needs vary from teacher to teacher. As you plan, work to individualize learning whenever possible.

Closing (5 minutes)

① Invite participants to sing the fourth stanza of "Go, Make of All Disciples" (*The United Methodist Hymnal*, 571).

② Lead the group in a closing prayer, thanking God for those who teach and asking for direction and vision as together you seek to make disciples in your congregation.

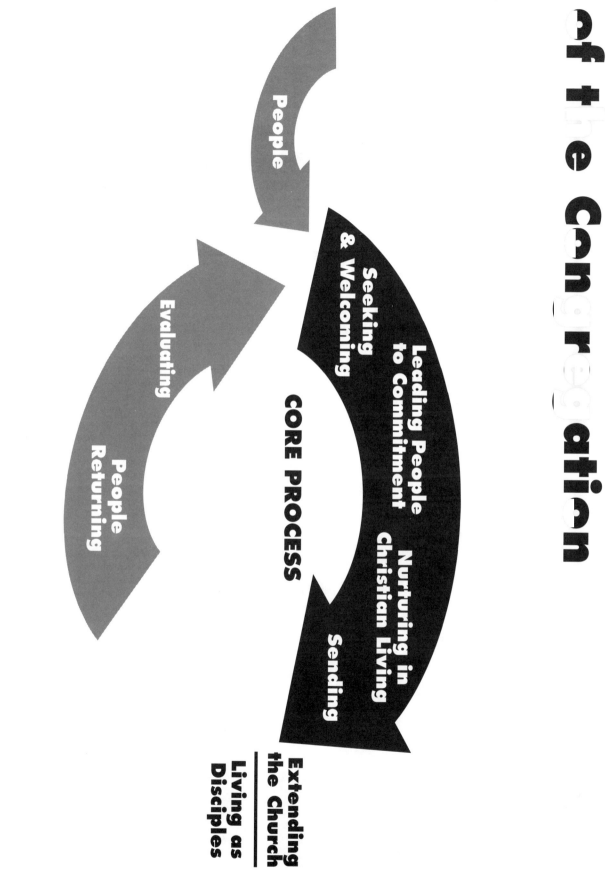

People

Evaluating

People Returning

CORE PROCESS

Seeking & Welcoming

Leading People to Commitment

Nurturing in Christian Living

Sending

Extending the Church

Living as Disciples

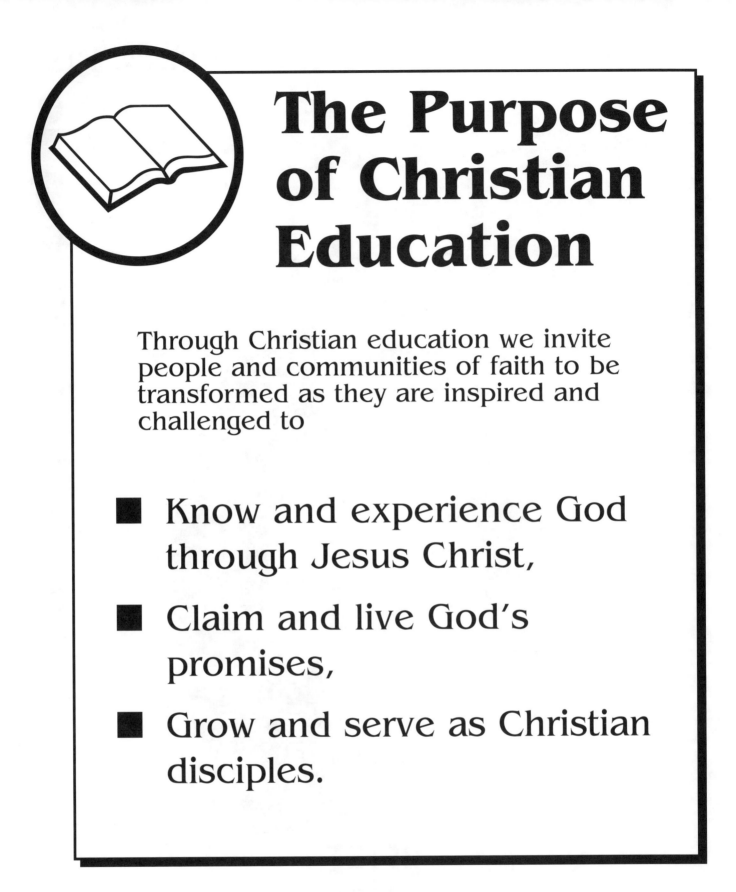

The Purpose of Christian Education

Through Christian education we invite people and communities of faith to be transformed as they are inspired and challenged to

- **Know and experience God through Jesus Christ,**

- **Claim and live God's promises,**

- **Grow and serve as Christian disciples.**

Biblical Reflection

After this the Lord appointed seventy others and sent them on ahead of him in pairs to every town and place where he himself intended to go. He said to them, "The harvest is plentiful, but the laborers are few; therefore ask the Lord of the harvest to send out laborers into his harvest. Go on your way. See, I am sending you out like lambs into the midst of wolves. Carry no purse, no bag, no sandals; and greet no one on the road. Whatever house you enter, first say, 'Peace to this house!' And if anyone is there who shares in peace, your peace will rest on that person; but if not, it will return to you. Remain in the same house, eating and drinking whatever they provide, for the laborer deserves to be paid. Do not move about from house to house. Whenever you enter a town and its people welcome you, eat what is set before you; cure the sick who are there, and say to them, 'The kingdom of God has come near to you.' But whenever you enter a town and they do not welcome you, go out into its streets and say, 'Even the dust of your town that clings to our feet, we wipe off in protest against you. Yet know this: the kingdom of God has come near.' I tell you, on that day it will be more tolerable for Sodom than for that town."

The seventy returned with joy, saying, "Lord, in your name even the demons submit to us!" He said to them, "I watched Satan fall from heaven like a flash of lightning. See, I have given you authority to tread on snakes and scorpions, and over all the power of the enemy; and nothing will hurt you. Nevertheless, do not rejoice at this, that the spirits submit to you, but rejoice that your names are written in heaven."

Bible Study

Group A: Theological Bible Study

Read the Scripture passage. Then think about these questions:

❶ What does the text say about God?

❷ What does the text say about human beings?

❸ What does the text say about the relationship between God and humans?

❹ What does the text say about the primary task of the congregation?

Discuss with members of your small group (as you are comfortable) your answers to the four questions.

Note: This method focuses on the content of Scripture—what the author wrote and what meaning (understanding or interpretation) can be derived from the passage.

Group B: Journaling

Ask a group member to read the Scripture passage aloud. Then, as individuals, spend a few minutes writing down your thoughts, feelings, ideas, and questions about the Scripture passage, particularly as they relate to the primary task of the congregation. Journaling can include letters to God, letters from God, or dialogues with God. Your thoughts might be as simple as a few words or sentences, or they might be complex and take up several pages. You might want to spend time later in reflecting further.

After group members have had a few minutes to journal, discuss as a group what you feel comfortable sharing from your journal.

Note: Members of this small group may wish to find a quiet corner in which to reflect and write.

Group C: Devotional Reading

Read the Scripture passage from the perspective of asking what it is that God has to say to you right now through this particular passage about the primary task of the congregation. Think about what distracts us from staying focused on the primary task (mission) of the church. You are reading not so much to understand the content as to hear and obey the message.

Read the text silently and reflect on it for a couple minutes. Then discuss in your group what you think God is saying to you.

Group D: Transformational Bible Study

Read the Scripture passage. Note any questions that come to mind as you read. Then respond in the group to the following questions:

❶ What truth does this passage teach about the primary task of the congregation? (What should we believe? How is our work defined?)

❷ How does the passage reveal misunderstanding or challenge our assumptions? (What should we avoid? What should our attitudes be?)

❸ What can be learned from this passage to help guide and transform us? (What should we value? How can we change?)

❹ What instructions does this passage give to direct our daily living? (How should we behave?)

❺ What do we need to do this week to put this passage into practice?

Note: This method focuses on how we can apply our learning to our daily living. It takes seriously the biblical mandate to "be transformed by the renewing of [our] minds" (Romans 12:2). Each person is invited to struggle for her or his own response.

Teaching and the Primary Task

As a teacher or small-group leader, you are instrumental in creating safe, respectful, healthy settings in which children, youth, and adults can grow and learn. You serve as a model, mentor, friend, and companion on the spiritual journeys of your group members. It is essential for you to understand how teaching and learning supports the church's primary task. The results of your reflection will provide your congregation with information for assisting teachers and small-group leaders in developing the knowledge and skills they need for fulfilling the primary task. Please read each statement. Then circle the number that best reflects where you are currently (1=not at all; 4=definitely). If you teach young children and/or nonreaders, some of the statements may not be applicable to your group.

Seek and Welcome People

1 2 3 4   ■ I contact group members when they are absent more than once.

1 2 3 4   ■ I recognize special occasions and accomplishments of our group members.

1 2 3 4   ■ I help people feel secure in new settings and with new people.

1 2 3 4   ■ I invite people who are not currently involved in our congregation to come to our class.

1 2 3 4   ■ Our group members are learning (continuing to learn) how to help people feel secure in new settings and with new people.

1 2 3 4   ■ Our group is a safe place to ask questions, discuss concerns, and learn from mistakes.

1 2 3 4   ■ In our group, people encounter others who listen to them.

Lead People to Commitment

1 2 3 4   ■ I regularly practice the spiritual disciplines of Bible study, prayer, worship, and acts of compassion.

1 2 3 4   ■ I regularly include the spiritual disciplines of Bible study, prayer, worship, and acts of compassion in our group meetings or classes.

1 2 3 4   ■ I feel comfortable sharing my faith with other people.

1 2 3 4   ■ I encourage group members to develop their ability to share their faith with other people.

1 2 3 4   ■ In our group, people can learn (continue to learn) to identify, name, and celebrate God's presence in their lives.

1 2 3 4   ■ In our group, people learn ways in which to respond to God's presence in their lives.

Nurture People in Christian Living

1 2 3 4 ■ I am familiar with most major people and events in the Bible.

1 2 3 4 ■ I know how to use Bible reference books to learn about the Bible.

1 2 3 4 ■ Our group members are familiar with most major people and events in the Bible.

1 2 3 4 ■ Our group members can easily find a passage in the Bible.

1 2 3 4 ■ Our group members have the knowledge and skills necessary to connect the biblical message to their daily lives.

1 2 3 4 ■ Our group members believe it is important to apply the teachings of the Bible to their personal and professional lives.

1 2 3 4 ■ I understand the developmental characteristics of the people in our group.

1 2 3 4 ■ I understand the variety of ways in which people learn.

1 2 3 4 ■ I use a variety of teaching/learning methods in our small group.

Equip People to Live as Servants of Christ

1 2 3 4 ■ Our group members believe it is important to serve others.

1 2 3 4 ■ Our group members volunteer time regularly in a service organization outside the church.

1 2 3 4 ■ Our group financially supports local, national, and worldwide mission projects.

1 2 3 4 ■ Our group members live their faith in their families.

1 2 3 4 ■ Our group members live their faith in their workplaces.

1 2 3 4 ■ Our group members encourage elected leaders to work for quality healthcare, education, housing, and employment for all people.

Building a **Learning Plan**

Review the information related to the primary task of the congregation and the purpose of Christian education. Think about the insights you gained through Bible study about the mission of the church. Examine your responses on your reflection sheet. Spend time listening to God.

Rate each of the following elements of teaching and small-group leadership in which you need to grow (10=most necessary; 1=least necessary).

Knowledge

____ Knowledge of the Bible

____ Knowledge about Christian discipleship

____ Knowledge of The United Methodist Church and church history

____ Knowledge and understanding of worship in the classroom or small group

____ Knowledge of how people learn

____ Knowledge of age-level characteristics

____ Other: _____ (Please list.)

Skills

____ Building healthy relationships in the group

____ Listening to other people

____ Asking effective questions

____ Storytelling

____ Using music in the class or small group

____ Leading discussion

____ Leading Bible study

____ Leading mission/service

____ Reflecting on mission/service

____ Leading prayer

____ Helping make connections between faith and life

____ Leading studies of contemporary issues

____ Other: _____ (Please list.)

What knowledge and skills do you want to develop or strengthen as you provide leadership for your class or small group? Check all of the following that apply:

Bible Study

____ Survey of the Old Testament

____ Survey of the New Testament

____ Book of the Bible: _____ (Name book.)

____ Biblical people: _____ (Name person.)

____ Biblical themes: _____ (Name theme.)

Knowledge of the Church

____ Christian worship

____ Important people in church history
_____ (Name person.)

____ United Methodist heritage

____ Other: _____ (Name topic.)

Spiritual Formation

____ Prayer

____ Bible-study skills

____ Fasting

____ Spiritual direction

____ Sharing faith

Contemporary Issues

____ Parenting

____ Marriage/relationships

____ Homelessness

____ Hunger

____ Poverty

____ Racial justice

____ People with disabilities

____ Education

____ Healthcare

____ HIV/AIDS

____ Aging

____ International conflicts/war

____ Other: _____ (Name issue.)

Mission/Outreach

____ Working in a homeless shelter or food pantry

____ Tutoring/literacy program for adults

____ Tutoring children or youth

____ Sports programs for children/youth

____ Visiting in a hospital/hospice

____ Visiting in a nursing home

____ Other: _____ (Name setting.)

Review all the topics that you checked. List your top three priorities below (1=top priority; 3=third priority).

1. (3 points)

2. (2 points)

3. (1 point)

With God's People

FOR THE **LEADER**

In highly mobile societies such as the United States, it is not difficult to find people who have relocated or made life adjustments at least once. People move because of a change in job, health, lifestyle, security, educational opportunities, or just for adventure. People move either by choice or out of necessity. We constantly hear of adults, children, and families being uprooted. If you have moved or experienced any change, you are probably familiar with feelings of disorientation, insecurity, or a sense of imbalance; of stress, anxiety, or a need for reorientation and adaptation. Changes can and do occur at the physical, emotional, material, intellectual, and spiritual levels. A quick survey of your community will most likely yield individuals and families who are going (or have gone through) that experience. Since people seem to be coming or going at different times and on different levels, there will always be strangers and foreigners, newcomers and outsiders among us. If you have ever been in that position, you know the value of being accepted and being anchored in a safe and secure community.

When we meet these people in our community, church, or workplace, what do we do to make them feel welcome and help them become acclimated to their new situation? If you were the newcomer, stranger, or guest, what would make you feel a part of the community or group? What would facilitate your easing into the new job, church, or neighborhood? What would you consider a hospitable environment? Within the context of a Christian community, what does it mean to offer and receive hospitality, as well as to create a hospitable environment?

Whenever we talk about hospitality, we are talking about a relationship between the one who offers it and the one who receives it. However, it is not a simple, one-way relationship. For both the giver and receiver, either as an individual or as a group, hospitality is a reciprocal process.

by Judith M. Bunyi

Secti⊕n 2

The Biblical Mandate

The Bible offers several passages that call us to practice hospitality—to offer it to the stranger among us. The Old Testament, particularly the Mosaic law, spells out our duties to strangers. The Hebrew people were commanded to offer hospitality to the sojourner, stranger, or alien. Exodus 22:21; Leviticus 19:34; and Deuteronomy 27:19 refer to the Israelites' duty to the traveler who was passing through and to the foreigner who had decided to live among them. God's chosen people were not to oppress or wrong strangers; they were to love them and ensure that justice was extended to them.

In the New Testament, both the apostle Paul and the writer of Hebrews urge communities of faith (Romans 12:13; Hebrews 13:2), as well as those aspiring for leadership in the church (1 Timothy 3:2; Titus 1:8), to be hospitable to strangers. The same message is echoed in 1 Peter 4:9. Most importantly, Jesus told his disciples about the Final Judgment and the measure by which we will be judged, one of which is whether or not we have practiced hospitality to strangers (Matthew 25:35, 43).

In biblical times, when travel along miles of dusty, lonely roads was mostly by foot, hospitality to strangers was a priority because one never knew when he or she would need the cordial reception of others. Hosts washed the feet of their guests and attended to their needs, after which they would invite the guests to join them at the table. Meeting the needs of the tired and hungry stranger or traveler was their primary way of showing hospitality. Even today, the same hospitality is still being practiced among nomadic tribes and in rural places and desert kingdoms in certain regions of the Middle East.

In light of the biblical mandate to practice hospitality, how are we to live it out as faithful disciples? Before we can offer gestures of friendship and warm welcome, before we can genuinely open our community or homes or lives to others who do not belong yet, we must first have a welcoming heart and mind. Do we have the spirit, passion, and conviction to receive people who may not be like us or share our beliefs? Are we ready to invite and take into our fellowship those who are different, perhaps in age, gender, looks, abilities, culture, profession, social standing, or even spiritual maturity?

A hospitable (as well as an inhospitable) heart and mind find their expressions through words and deeds. If we do not honestly believe in creating a hospitable place, where people can feel safe and accepted for who they are, the phoniness of our attempts will be exposed sooner or later. If we believe in it, that will also show.

The Practice of Hospitality

Others can easily see through our actions and make judgments about our sincerity. They are likely to put more weight on how we behave; therefore, they will doubt our verbal message when our actions contradict our words of welcome. When our words and actions complement each other, our gestures of hospitality become credible. Therefore, if we have the mind of Christ and a heart and attitude of hospitality, and if we wholeheartedly accept the scriptural command and follow the examples set for us, then that will translate into a language that can easily be read as graciousness and goodwill. What we say and how we say it convey our interest in the needs of others.

When our words and actions complement each other, our gestures of hospitality become credible.

Since genuine hospitality is other-centered and other-directed, rather than self-centered and self-serving, it would be good for us to take the time to get to know the other person. If we do, we will better understand their perspective, where they are coming from, and the needs they might have. When we start to focus outward, our words and actions begin to demonstrate our readiness to receive them and our willingness to hear them out. This will show our resolve to include them in the circle, to make them feel comfortable, and to give them permission to exercise their gifts.

Some of those who have visited my country, the Philippines, have noted the Filipino hospitality. Foreigners or not, unexpected guests who happen to arrive around mealtime will always be invited to eat with the family or host. It doesn't matter whether the guest is a new acquaintance, a long-time friend, or kin—the hosts will be happy to share the table with him or her. It is one way of saying to the guest, "You are now one of us. Consider us your family and this your own home." If there is not enough food, there is no question as to who will make the sacrifice in order to accommodate and feed the guests. The best portion is always offered to (and expected to be accepted by) the visitors. If the guests have come from a far distance and appear to need overnight accommodations, the family will readily give their best room and bed for the visitors' use. However humble and meager our resources may be, the best is always to be reserved for our guests. We take great pains (and pleasure) in making sure that our guests are comfortable and made to feel welcome. If you come at a time other than mealtime, you will be offered snacks and drinks.

Being hospitable involves one's total being. However, before we can come to the point of living and breathing it and before it becomes second nature to us, it has to be practiced in an intentional way. Hospitality is not a one-time event. It does not begin and end with a handshake, a smile, and the words "I'm glad you're here."

It is an attitude and a lifestyle in which words and actions are not only peppered with friendliness, kindness, compassion, and consideration for others, but the totality of who and what we are spells *w-e-l-c-o-m-e* and is sustained over our lifetime. Thinking about how others feel is important. Words and actions that affirm their personhood, that recognize their gifts and talents, that express equality and acceptance, and that build up community will lead to more-positive relationships with others and help create a more-welcoming environment.

The Context of Hospitality

It is easy to say, "I like everybody. Everyone's always welcome to come and join us anytime." One way to test it is to look at your small groups. We have a variety of small-group settings in our churches. Some are created for specific ministries and tasks, such as the choir or worship, the trustees, the finance committee, staff-parish relations committee, evangelism, mission, outreach, and other short-term task forces (such as the building committee). There are groups that are formed for purposes of learning and discipleship, nurture and fellowship, accountability and support, or sharing a common interest.

Does your group pay attention to the needs of the newcomer? If so, how?

I invite you to take a closer look at the nature of your group. Specifically, choose a group that has open membership (there are no specific qualifications, unlike a group such as the board of trustees that is elected by the charge conference).

Take, for example, your Sunday school class, youth group, Bible study group, prayer group, or fellowship group for seniors or singles. How open are you to newcomers? If you were an outsider visiting the group for the first time, would you feel comfortable sitting anywhere and engaging any member in conversation? Will members of the group readily and gladly receive you? Or is there an unwritten rule that dictates who sits where and by whom? Are there cliques that are apparent and hard to penetrate? Does your group pay attention to the needs of the newcomer? If so, how?

If you were the facilitator or leader of the group, how would you make sure that the newcomer—every member for that matter—would feel welcome, not just during the first visit but every time he or she is there? How would you enable the group to create a friendly and inviting setting? How would you encourage all participants to be open not only to new people but also to new ideas without compromising biblical truths?

Critical Skills

When interacting face-to-face with others, one of the ways we can practice hospitality is through listening—actively, attentively, and supportively. Of the four communication skills (listening, speaking, reading, and writing), listening is the first skill we learn as a child. It is also the skill we often use, yet the one in which we receive the least training. In school we took specific courses in order to learn how to read, write, and speak. At best, we were made to realize through admonitions—"Sit down and listen," "Keep quiet and pay attention," "How many times do I have to tell you to listen?" and "You are not listening to me"—the importance of listening.

What is listening, anyway? Listening is a complex process that involves not just the passive reception of messages. There is more to it than just sitting and physically hearing the sounds and words of the other person. When we listen actively and attentively, it means that all our faculties are involved. In face-to-face interpersonal communication, we also hear with our eyes the nonverbal language that accompanies the verbal message. In order to do that accurately, we need to work hard to avoid the various forms of distractions that may distort our reception and interpretation of the message. Distractions that are external to the listener may include noise, interruptions, extreme temperatures, and the mannerisms or appearance of the speaker. Internal distractions may include fatigue, daydreaming, prejudices and biases, and physical and emotional conditions. It is important to be aware of these distractions and to work at controlling or keeping them to a minimum while listening to the speaker. Being attentive to all the cues from the speaker will help us in the process of assigning meaning to what we hear.

Even when we are able to focus and concentrate on the speaker and the message, we sometimes encounter problems in interpreting the message. Each person, based on his or her experiences and learnings, has a set of emotionally charged words. These words or phrases raise a red flag for the listener, whether or not the speaker intended them to do that.

Listening, after all, is hard work. If we are to be effective listeners, we need to invest the time to learn and practice effective listening skills.

When this happens, we can do one or several of the following steps: We can let the speaker finish the sentence, withhold our reaction until the end, refrain from constructing our arguments while we wait for our turn, ask questions for clarification, check our perception of the message with the speaker, be open to correction and to other views, be tentative with our own opinion, learn to separate fact from opinion, resist jumping to conclusions, and focus on the issue rather than on the person. I know that these are easier to say than to do. Listening, after all, is hard work. If we are to be effective listeners, we need to invest the time to learn and practice effective listening skills. By taking the time to listen and understand others, we will be able to provide the appropriate feedback, which will make others feel that they have been heard. When others feel that they have been heard, we have created a warm, accepting environment.

Listening is also a message in itself. Aside from being mentally engaged while listening and providing appropriate verbal feedback, we can also show our support and respect for the speaker through our posture (forward lean), direct eye contact, appropriate facial expression, and head nods (to indicate either understanding or agreement or both). Vocal expressions such as "Uh-huh" and not interrupting or putting down the speaker are other ways. Through these channels, we are able to tell others that they are worth our time and energy and that they are part of a supportive community. Often, what a speaker needs is just a listening ear, but sometimes we cannot resist the temptation to provide answers for every question or concern the other person may have.

Of course, we can also send the message of lack of interest or respect through our body language, but that would not help build up our brothers and sisters as people of worth. Consequently, it will not build Christian community, and the community will not be a hospitable one. If so, we run counter to our calling as Christian disciples.

When we gather and meet in small groups, we have the opportunity to explore and grow in our faith together. As we study the Scriptures together and learn what it means to be disciples, as we pray for each other, as we share and listen to each other's faith stories, as we support and nurture each other, as we accept each other in spite of our differences, we fulfill the biblical mandate to practice hospitality. We are building a Christian community, where Christ's love abides and is lived out.

Christian community is also built when our trust and respect for each other are also deepened. Through sharing and self-disclosure, listening and giving feedback, we learn more about each other and are better able to understand and care for one another. It is important to remember that trust and respect will continue to grow strong when confidentiality is observed and guarded. It is part of being hospitable. It helps if members of the group draw up a covenant that includes how they will observe confidentiality.

Spiritual Gifts

A hospitable community that is characterized by pervading openness and friendly reception is a fertile ground for the manifestation of "the fruit of the Spirit...love, joy, peace, patience, kindness, generosity, faithfulness, gentleness,

A hospitable community that is characterized by pervading openness and friendly reception is a fertile ground for the manifestation of "the fruit of the Spirit."

and self-control" (Galatians 5:22). On the other hand, this fruit also contributes toward creating a hospitable setting. It works both ways; one cannot exist without the other. Both are evidence of growth toward spiritual maturity, as well as Christian discipleship.

Because the fruit of the Spirit flourishes and ushers in a climate of receptivity, members of the Christian community are also able to freely explore and exercise the different gifts that God has given them. All our gifts, talents, and abilities come from God and have been apportioned according to God's grace. We vary in our giftedness, and we are to use those gifts in serving God and others. As such, we do not have the right to put others down and put ourselves high on a pedestal, or vice versa. Instead, in a spirit and attitude of hospitality, we should welcome the contributions of others and consider theirs on equal footing with our own gifts and abilities, knowing that we all need and complement one another. In the exercise of our different gifts and in living out the fruit of the Spirit in our lives and community, we need to remember that we all belong to one body and are all united under the lordship of Christ (1 Corinthians 12:12-31). As Christ's disciples, we are called to be witnesses to God's saving grace and love. A community of faith that accepts people for who they are and invites them to be part of a life-transforming experience in the Spirit has learned what true discipleship means.

Helpful Resources

Leading Small Groups: Basic Skills for Church and Community Organizations, by Nathan W. Turner (Valley Forge: Judson Press, 1997).

Nine Keys to Effective Small Group Leadership: How Lay Leaders Can Establish Dynamic and Healthy Cells, Classes, or Teams, by Carl F. George (Mansfield, PA: Kingdom Publishing, 1997).

Seven Tools for Building Effective Groups, by Jeffrey Arnold (Colorado Springs: NavPress Publishing Company, 1997).

Small Group Idea Book: Resources to Enrich Community, Worship, Prayer, Nurture, Outreach, edited by Cindy Bunch (Downers Grove, IL: InterVarsity Press, 1996).

Teacher Development Workshop:
Creating a Hospitable Environment

Purpose

The purpose of this workshop is to help teachers and leaders of small groups understand the biblical foundation for creating a hospitable environment and explore ways by which we can be a welcoming, accepting, and hospitable community.

Scripture

Romans 12:3-8 and 14:1–15:13

Time

This session is designed to last approximately one and a half hours.

Materials

- Bibles
- Hymnals
- Construction paper
- Scissors
- Photocopies (one per person) of the following:
- "Questions for Study and Reflection" (page 32)
- "Rating My Listening Skills" (page 33)
- Photocopies (two per person) of "Circles of Influence" (page 34)
- Pencils
- Newsprint
- Felt-tip markers
- Masking tape

Preparation

- Review the workshop plan and adapt it, as necessary, to your congregation.
- Write the purpose statement of this workshop on newsprint.
- Photocopy the handouts (pages 32–34).
- Gather the supplies listed above.

Workshop Outline

- Gathering and Group Building (15 minutes)
- Bible Study and Group Reflection (25 minutes)
- Evaluating Listening Skills (20 minutes)
- Developing a Plan for Hospitality (25 minutes)
- Closing (5 minutes)

Workshop Plan

Gathering and Group Building (15 minutes)

1 As group members arrive, ask them to cut a shape from construction paper and to make it into a nametag. Encourage them to decorate the nametag.

2 When everyone is seated, ask the participants to introduce themselves by stating their name and telling why they chose the shape and color and drew the decorations they did for their nametag. Be sure that each person is given an equal amount of time.

3 Present the objective of the workshop (written on newsprint) and lead the opening prayer.

Bible Study and Group Reflection (25 minutes)

1 Divide the group into smaller discussion groups of from three to five people. Give each person a photocopy of "Questions for Study and Reflection" (page 32) and ask them to use the questions as a guide for their discussion.

2 Gather the group together and invite them to tell about their insights from their group discussion. List on newsprint the ways in which others have modeled a welcoming spirit and attitude.

Evaluating Listening Skills (20 minutes)

1 Remind the group that one of the primary ways we offer hospitality is through listening. Ask the participants to think back to a recent experience they had listening to someone else, such as a coworker, family member, or friend.

2 Give each person a photocopy of "Rating My Listening Skills" (page 33) and ask them to rate themselves ("Me" column) based on the experience they have just remembered. Then ask them to imagine that they are the person to whom they were listening. Have them rate how they think that person ("Others" column) would have rated their listening skills. Have them add up both columns of numbers and compare them.

3 Ask the participants to circle the items that have the lowest numbers. Use the information in the section "Critical Skills" (pages 26–27) to lead a discussion on helpful listening skills. Use the following questions as a springboard for discussion:
■ What irritates you when someone is listening to you?
■ What makes you feel as if someone has listened to you?
■ What would make you a better listener?

4 Invite the participants to list at the bottom of "Rating My Listening Skills" three things they can do to improve their listening skills. Encourage them to take the list home and place it where they will see it frequently.

Developing a Plan for Hospitality (25 minutes)

❶ Give each person two photocopies of "Circles of Influence" (page 34). Ask them to read the information on the sheet and to label one copy "Me" and the other "Our Group." Ask each person to write on the sheet labeled "Me" the names of people within their circle of influence to whom they will offer hospitality this week. Next have them write the names of those outside their circle to whom they can offer hospitality. Then have them list with each name what they intend to do to offer hospitality to that person.

❷ Ask the group the following questions and have them write their answers on the sheet labeled "Our Group."
- Who are the people within our group's circle of influence?
- Who are the people outside our group's circle of influence?
- What are specific ways we can extend hospitality to both of these groups? (For other suggestions, review "Critical Skills," on pages 26–27.)
- How can we be accountable to one another to ensure that we carry through on our plans?

Closing (5 minutes)

❶ Invite participants to offer prayers (silently or aloud) for those to whom you, as individuals and as a group, will offer hospitality.

❷ Close with an appropriate chorus or song. Possibilities include the following hymns from *The United Methodist Hymnal:* "Where Charity and Love Prevail" (549), "Help Us Accept Each Other" (560), and "Like the Murmur of the Dove's Song" (544).

Study and Reflection

Read Romans 12:3-8 and 14:1–15:13.
Use the following questions to help you explore these passages.

1 Who is the author of this letter? To whom is the author addressing the letter?

2 What are the primary messages of these passages?

3 Who is supposed to practice hospitality?

4 To whom should hospitality be offered?

5 How is hospitality to be lived out?

6 Why do believers need to offer hospitality?

7 How do these Scripture passages speak to your life as an individual and to our life as a group?

8 Who are the people who have offered you hospitality? How have they modeled a welcoming spirit and attitude?

9 How practical is it to offer hospitality to strangers today?

Rating My Listening Skills

Use the following scale to rate yourself as a listener. In the second column rate how you think others would rate you.

1 I never do this.
2 I seldom do this.
3 I do this about half the time.
4 I do this often.
5 I do this all the time.

Me	Others	
_____	_____	■ I try to minimize external distractions (television, radio, extreme temperatures) when I am listening.
_____	_____	■ I try to minimize internal distractions (fatigue, daydreaming, personal biases) when I am listening.
_____	_____	■ I provide helpful nonverbal cues (head-nodding, eye contact, leaning forward) when I am listening.
_____	_____	■ I provide helpful verbal feedback when I am listening (rephrasing what I have heard, asking appropriate questions).
_____	_____	■ I don't interrupt the speaker when he or she says something with which I don't agree.
_____	_____	■ I don't try to provide answers or solve the problems for the person to whom I am listening.
_____	_____	■ I pay attention to nonverbal cues from the person to whom I am listening.
_____	_____	■ I try to focus on what the person is saying, rather than thinking about what I want to say to the person.
_____	_____	■ I avoid body language that indicates a lack of interest (toe-tapping, fidgeting, turning away from the speaker).

Total _____ _____

Three things I can do to improve my listening skills.

1

2

3

Influence

Circles of

In your day-to-day life, you come into contact with a wide variety of people. Because of your relationship with them, many of these people are influenced by your words and actions. These are people who are within your circle of influence.

There are others with whom you come into contact, but have less of an influence on. These people are outside your circle of influence. As an individual and as a group, you can offer hospitality to both those within and outside your circle of influence.

With Your Experience

A growing faith asks important questions and seeks complex, relevant answers. Our important questions of today are similar to the questions our biblical ancestors asked: How do we know that we are being faithful? How can we see the activity of God in everyday life? What would God have me do with my life? How these questions are answered is vitally important to our families, churches, cities, and nations. We want to be open to God's presence and activity in our lives. Our biblical ancestors dared to ask these important questions. Their questioning and thinking made them faithful people. One way for us to ask these important questions is to pause, to stop. In our hurried, busy world, we must make time to reflect on these questions with other Christians. Theological reflection is taking time to think, question, and dialogue with people about God and our relationship with God. Theological reflection is also something that is done quite naturally, even among parents and children.

One night I was driving home with my friend Angela and her children (Alex, Amy, and Suzie) after spending a weekend together in the mountains. We were about two hours from home when a red light flashed on the car's dashboard, indicating that something was wrong with the engine. We pulled to the side of the highway and discovered a broken belt when we checked under the hood. We knew it was unsafe to drive the car with a broken belt and had no way to ask for help, so we stood on the side of the highway waiting. In about twenty minutes, a tow truck pulled up behind us. The driver had the belt we needed in his truck, and we were back on the road again in about ten minutes. As we pulled back onto the highway, I mentioned how wonderful it was that God had intervened and fixed our car. Nine-year-old Suzie said that God had not fixed the car—the tow truck man had. My friend and I talked to Suzie and the other children about how God sends people to help us, especially when we are in crisis. We asked the children if they knew any stories in the Bible of events similar to our story. The children mentioned Mary

by N. Lynne Westfield

Section 3

and Joseph, when they needed a room on Christmas Eve and the innkeeper helped them by giving them a stable in which to sleep. Then they mentioned the Samaritan man who found an injured man at the side of the road and cared for him by taking him to a safe place. The children could see better how God wants us to help one another like the tow truck man had helped us, like the innkeeper had helped Mary and Joseph, like the Samaritan had helped the injured man. My friend and I recognized once again the fact that God sends people to help in times of trouble and expects each of us to help others. Our conversation was a theological reflection that lasted the rest of the way home.

Theological reflection is more than simply discussing or debating issues of faith, more than trying to discern the will of God in our lives. Theological reflection helps to suggest new actions, new behaviors that are ethical, responsible, and faithful. A congregation or class that spends all its time in conversation and never acts on any decisions is like a trumpet without a mouthpiece or a car without tires. Conversely, a church that does ministry or programming without taking time to reflect is just spinning its wheels or guessing. Theological reflection compels people to action after the conversations, and it compels them to have conversations about previous actions. If we are to grow in faith, there must be action and reflection.

The adventure in the car with my friend and her children was an informal way of doing theological reflection. The workshop in this section is a formal way of doing theological reflection. The form of theological reflection suggested in this section is called story-linking, which is an ancient way of hearing stories of our ordinary lives with stories from the Bible. When we hear the two stories together, it is amazing how similar the experiences of faith are. (To learn more about story-linking, read *Soul Stories: African American Christian Education*.)

The biblical story of this lesson focuses on Chapter 16 of Genesis. It is the story of Hagar, Sarai and Abram's slave. Hagar gives us an excellent example about the messiness of faith and the courage it takes to be a disciple of God. The story of Hagar is one that is not often told, but it is vitally important if we are to work for peace and justice.

Helpful Resources

Soul Stories: African American Christian Education, by Anne Streaty Wimberly (Nashville: Abingdon Press, 1994).

Teaching Scripture From an African-American Perspective, by Joseph V. Crockett (Nashville: Discipleship Resources, 1990).

The Art of Theological Reflection, by Patricia O'Connell Killen and John de Beer (New York: Crossroad Publishing Company, 1994).

Theological reflection helps to suggest new actions, new behaviors that are ethical, responsible, and faithful.

Teacher Development Workshop:
Practicing Theological Reflection

Purpose

The purpose of this workshop is to help teachers and small-group leaders do the six-step process of story-linking and see issues of peace and justice within their own lives.

Scripture

Genesis 16

Time

This session is designed to last from three to five hours. It could also be used in a one- or two-day retreat.

Materials

- Candle and matches (optional)
- Bibles (several translations)
- Cassette tape recorder and cassette tape (optional)
- Photocopies of the written personal story (optional)
- Person as storyteller for the personal story (optional)
- Newsprint
- Felt-tip markers
- Masking tape
- Photocopies (one per person) of the following:
  "What Would God Have Us Do Today?" (page 42)
  "Six Steps for Theological Reflection" (page 43)
  "Process for Individual Reflection" (page 44)
- Pencils
- Modeling clay (optional)
- Writing paper
- Fabrics and props for pantomime (optional)

Preparation

- Review the workshop plan and adapt it, as necessary, to your congregation.
- Write the purpose statement of this workshop on newsprint.
- Photocopy the handouts (pages 42–44).
- Gather the supplies listed above.
- For Step 1: Telling the Personal Story
  Selecting a Personal Story: Ask a person who will be attending the workshop to prepare a personal story of a critical incident when he or she was dealt with harshly and unjustly and wanted to run away. (Or you may prepare a personal story for the group.) He or she may have run away physically, as well as emotionally and spiritually. Ask that person to write the story for others to read or to record it on a cassette tape for

the group to listen to. The story should be no longer than two pages in length or fifteen minutes recorded on tape.

The Storytelling: Decide before class how the story will be presented. If the storyteller is writing the story, have photocopies of the story so that each person can read along. If the story is to be played on cassette, have the tape and a tape player. If the person is going to tell the story in first person, rehearse with the person before the workshop.

■ For Step 3: Telling the Biblical Story: Genesis 16
Have needed supplies ready: variety of biblical translations, props or fabrics for the pantomiming, and modeling clay.

Workshop Outline

■ Gathering and Group Building (15–20 minutes)
■ Step 1: Telling the Personal Story (20–40 minutes)
■ Step 2: Delving Into the Personal Story (20–45 minutes)
■ Step 3: Telling the Biblical Story: Genesis 16 (30–40 minutes)
■ Step 4: Delving Into the Biblical Story (20–45 minutes)
■ Step 5: Listening as Both Stories Speak (20–45 minutes)
■ Step 6: What Would God Have Us Do Today? (30–45 minutes)
■ Closing (15–20 minutes)

Workshop Plan

Gathering and Group Building (15–20 minutes)
(Choose one or all of the following options.)

❶ **Simple Introductions**
Invite each person to introduce him or herself and briefly say why he or she has chosen to be present for this experience.

❷ **Three Might-Be Truths**
Invite each person to tell three things about him or herself—two things that are true and one thing that is not true. The group should then guess which one of the three items is not true.

❸ **Prayer Circle**
Gather in a circle, light a candle, and pray together. Keep the candle lit for the entire learning workshop; then gather around it for the closing prayer.

Step 1: Telling the Personal Story (20–40 minutes)
❶ Review the purpose of the workshop (written on newsprint), letting participants know that they will be learning a process that will help them reflect on their personal experiences from a perspective of faith.

❷ Have the volunteer tell the personal story, play the cassette recording of the story, or have the participants read the photocopy of the story. Invite the workshop participants to listen closely without asking questions until the story is completely told.

3 After the entire story is told, invite the workshop participants to ask clarifying question only. They are not to fix the situation, give advice, or judge the situation or story. They may ask only questions that will help them understand the issues and details of the story.

Step 2: Delving Into the Personal Story (20–45 minutes)

1 Remind the group that it is vitally important that they not judge the person or events of the story at this point in the process. Suspend judgment during this discussion.

2 Begin by brainstorming a "menu" of emotions. List at least one hundred feelings (happy, sad, confused, lonely, fearful, and so forth), and leave the list posted during the discussion. This will help to get the juices flowing about possible emotions and will assist the learners in thinking about more-complex emotions.

3 Respond to the following questions as a whole group or in groups of threes or fours:
- What feelings are specifically mentioned in the story? What feelings are implied? When you hear the story, how do you feel?
- If this story were in the newspaper, what would the headline read? (List as many as possible.) If you were a lawyer (or a team of lawyers) who had to present this case before a judge who wanted only "the facts," what would you present? Formulate the case you would present to the judge.
- What does this story and its circumstances smell like, taste like, sound like, look like? What is a symbol of its texture or feel? Using your intuition and imagination, what does it make you feel like on the inside? When you were in similar circumstances, what image, metaphor, or symbol might represent that situation?

Step 3: Telling the Biblical Story: Genesis 16 (30–40 minutes)

1 Have a variety of Bible translations available. Quickly and briefly review what people know about Abram and Sarai up to but not including Genesis 16.

2 Read Genesis 16 aloud together.

3 Tell the story at least two more times. Select one of the following methods to retell the story together, or create your own way.
- **Pantomime**
  Assign people a character in the story to portray. In pantomime, only the narrator speaks. The actors must use their bodies to tell the story and convey the emotions of the characters. The characters are Narrator, Sarai, Abram, Hagar, Angel of the Lord, Ishmael. If you have fabrics and props, ask the participants to use them.
- **Modeling clay**
  Let each person select some modeling clay. Ask them to use the clay and to feel the emotions of the characters while listening to you retell the story. They may actually create something with the clay, or they may simply manipulate the clay while listening. Talk briefly about any new insights concerning the story.

A Faithful **Future**

Step 4: Delving Into the Biblical Story (20–45 minutes)

❶ Refocus the group by reminding them that they must continue to suspend judgment during this discussion.

❷ Respond to the following questions as a whole group or in groups of threes or fours:
- What feelings are specifically mentioned in the story? What feelings are implied? When you hear the story, how do you feel?
- If this story were in the newspaper, what would the headline read? (List as many as possible.) If you were a lawyer (or a team of lawyers) who had to present this case before a judge who wanted only "the facts," what would you present? Formulate the case you would present to the judge.
- What does this story and its circumstances smell like, taste like, sound like, look like? What is a symbol of its texture or feel? Using your intuition and imagination, what does it make you feel like on the inside? When you were in similar circumstances, what image, metaphor, or symbol might represent that situation?

Note: If you broke down into small groups, have the groups report their insights and fresh ideas to the whole group. It is important that all three aspects (feelings, facts, metaphors) of this inquiry be covered and reported back.

Step 5: Listening as Both Stories Speak (20–45 minutes)

Invite the participants to compare and contrast the biblical story and the personal story. Use the following questions and statements to stimulate discussion:
- List the similarities between the two stories. (Use the reports concerning feelings, facts, and metaphors to help you.)
- List important aspects of each story that you do not see in the other story.
- List the differences between the two stories.
- How does the personal story illuminate the biblical story, and how does the biblical story bring insight to the personal story? How does each story push and pull the other story? What does one story have to say to the other story?
- Now that you have heard both stories, what new insights do you see?

Step 6: What Would God Have Us Do Today? (30–45 minutes)

❶ Give each person a photocopy of "What Would God Have Us Do Today?" (page 42) and invite each person to spend time alone answering the questions on the sheet. Let them know that there will be a time for discussion, but that they will not be turning in the papers. No one else will see what they have written.

❷ Invite volunteers to tell about insights or decisions they have made.

❸ Give each person a photocopy of "Six Steps for Theological Reflection" (page 43) and "Process for Individual Reflection" (page 44). Explain that "Six Steps for Theological Reflection" summarizes the process they just experienced, and that "Process for Individual Reflection" illustrates other ways they can continue to use the Scripture to help inform and transform their actions. Encourage the participants to think about how they can create ongoing opportunities for theological reflection in their daily lives.

Closing (15–20 minutes)
(Choose one or all of the following options.)

❶ Speak Words of Appreciation

Invite people to say anything they need to say about the experience to feel complete. They may want to voice words of thanks or blessing at this time.

❷ Write Group Poems

Give each person a piece of writing paper and a pencil. Fold the paper like an accordion, making spaces for the number of people in the group. For example, if there are nine people, fold the paper nine times. Once the paper is folded, it should look like a fan or accordion. Have the group sit in a circle, and have each person write one insight in the first fold of the paper. Now ask everyone to pass their paper to the right. The next person should read the insight and write in the next fold an insight, truth, question, or a few words concerning the experience. The paper should then be passed to the right. Each time the paper is passed, the person may read only the words the previous person wrote. Do this until everyone has written one line on all the papers. Now have the participants unfold the papers and take turns reading aloud the poems about this shared experience, which were created by the group.

❸ Gather Around the Candle

Have the group gather in a circle around the candle and invite volunteers to offer prayers about the experience.

Have Us Do Today?

What Would God

Consider: (a) your personal life, (b) your role as a teacher or small-group leader, (c) the ministries of your local church, (d) your family and friends, (e) other aspects of your life. Ask yourself what you have gained as a result of the new insight.

 1 What will I continue to do?

 2 What will I stop doing?

 3 What will I start doing?

4 What unanswered questions or concerns do I still have? (List three or four.)

5 What new behaviors or actions will I begin? Who will I tell so that they might assist me in my behavioral change?

Theological Reflection

Step 1:
Remember a Personal Story

It is possible to reflect on nearly any experience. Those experiences that often provide the richest fields for reflection are ones that evoke strong emotions, cause us to be uncomfortable, or are particularly significant life events.

Step 2:
Delve Into the Personal Story

- Identify feelings, both spoken and implied, that the story evoked.
- Identify the key facts in the story.
- Use your intuition and imagination to experience the smells, tastes, sounds, textures, and sights of the story.
- Identify symbols, images, and metaphors that represent the story.

Step 3:
Remember a Biblical Story

- Remember a biblical story that reminds you in some way of the personal story. Don't spend a lot of time trying to discover the perfect biblical story to go with the personal story. Go with your general impressions and hunches. The goal of this process is to allow life stories and biblical stories to speak to one another. Often, biblical stories that on the surface seem only marginally related to the personal story become rich with meaning as the process unfolds.
- Read the biblical story from several different translations.
- Retell the story using words, drama, sculpture, music, or other creative media.

Step 4:
Delve Into the Biblical Story

- Identify feelings, both spoken and implied, that the story evoked.
- Identify the key facts in the story.
- Use your intuition and imagination to experience the smells, tastes, sounds, textures, and sights of the story.
- Identify symbols, images, and metaphors that represent the story.

Step 5:
Listen as Both Stories Speak

- List the similarities between the two stories, using the reports concerning feelings, facts, and metaphors to help you.
- List important aspects of each story that you do not see in the other story.
- List the differences between the two stories.
- Describe how the personal story illuminates the biblical story, and how the biblical story brings insight to the personal story. How does each story push and pull the other story? What does one story have to say to the other story?
- Name new insights that you see.

Step 6:
What Would God Have Us Do Today?

- Based on the conversation you have had about a personal story and the Scripture, consider how your life will be transformed. Use the questions listed on the handout "What Would God Have Us Do Today?" to guide your thinking.

Individual Reflection

Process for

1. Create a Story Action-Line

Read the story of Hagar (Genesis 16) thoroughly. Make an action-line of the story. Take as much time as you need for this project. It might take you an hour, a day, or many days to complete. Write down each aspect of the story on a separate line of your paper. Record each movement, each plot twist, each time a character does an action in the story. Now look at the action-line you created, taking time to examine each action of the story. Consider the actions, motivations, consequences of each character. See yourself in all of these actions and as all of the characters. Ask yourself when you have done any of these actions, or when any of these circumstances or feelings have been part of your life. Record your responses beside each of the action-lines you created. Ask yourself how your response was similar to or different from the plot line of the story. What insights into your own journey can you gain from Hagar's story? What is God calling you to be or become, do or do differently now that you know the story of Hagar? Using your action-line as a reference for the plot, write a contemporary version of Hagar's story.

2. Keep a Diary for Thirty, Sixty, Ninety Days

In the story of Hagar, the angel asks her, "Where have you come from and where are you going?" (Genesis 16:8). Set a specific amount of time to keep this diary—thirty, sixty, or ninety days. Each day record in your diary the relevant response to the following questions: Where have you come from? Where are you going? Be specific and concrete with your answers, and/or be imaginative, creative, poetic. At the end of the designated time, reread your diary for insights to the questions of where are you going and from where you have come.

3. Name God and Pray Using the New Names

Hagar is the first person in the Bible to name God *El-roi*, which means "God of seeing" or "God who sees." Take seven to ten days to complete the following task: Make a list of no less than one hundred names that honor and revere God. Once your list is complete, select three or four names that are less familiar to you. Write prayers calling God by these new names. Sit quietly after each prayer and listen for an answer to your prayer.

with the World

FOR THE **LEADER**

Wishing to test Jesus, a lawyer asked, "Which commandment in the law is the greatest?" Jesus answered, "You shall love the Lord your God with all your heart, and with all your soul, and with all your mind.... You shall love your neighbor as yourself. On these two commandments hang all the law and the prophets" (Matthew 22:35-40).

Almost eighteen hundred years later, John Wesley called for early Methodists to practice acts of piety (prayer, Bible study, worship, fasting) and acts of mercy (acting with compassion and working for justice). Piety wed to mercy echoes Jesus' answer concerning the Great Commandment.

Near the end of the twentieth century, Christian educators were reminding us that mature Christians have a faith that echoes Jesus' answer. In a 1990 report released by Search Institute of Minneapolis, mature faith was defined as faith with a strong vertical dimension (a well-tended relationship with God) and a strong horizontal dimension (acting with compassion and working for justice). After surveying some 11,000 adults in six denominations, Search Institute reported that about one-third of adults in these mainline churches have an undeveloped faith. (Their faith is not strong vertically or horizontally.) The survey revealed that about one-third of adults have a one-dimensional faith. (They invest time nurturing a relationship with God and give little thought to serving neighbor, or they seek to live with concern and compassion for others, but do not take time to nurture their own spirits through such disciplines as prayer and Bible study.)

According to the Search report, about one-third of the adults in mainline denominations are equipped with a mature faith (where love of God and love of neighbor are deeply intertwined).

by Joyce Brown

Section 4

The need is urgent. Mainline denominations need teachers and small-group leaders who can continue to grow in faithfulness and who can challenge others to faithfulness.

Good teachers talk about modeling behavior because it is effective for teaching and leading in the Christian church. Teachers who walk the path of faithfulness inspire others to consider the faith-filled journey. Most of us can name a mentor or two from our past who challenged us to become what God intends us to be. The challenge may have been issued in words. Or it may have been issued in lifestyle: We recognized faithful living in another and were challenged to respond in faithful ways to God.

Most of us do not teach long before we realize that we have been entrusted with an awesome responsibility. In our desire to be evangelists (messengers of the good news), we have exposed ourselves to being exposed. We challenge our fellow learners to grapple with the biblical mandate for mission, knowing that our own behavior either strengthens or weakens the challenge. The wise among us soon learn that we need the daily discipline of holy habits. We learn that spending time in prayer and study is a weight-lifting exercise. We are toned and strengthened and stretched to walk the way of the faithful.

Teachers who walk the path of faithfulness inspire others to consider the faith-filled journey.

Helpful Resources

Front Porch Tales: Warm-Hearted Stories of Family, Faith, Laughter, and Love (1997) and *Home Town Tales: Recollections of Kindness, Peace, and Joy* (1998), both by Philip Gulley (Sisters, OR: Multnomah Publishers, Inc.). Written by a Quaker minister, these books will help you discover spiritual gifts in the lives of ordinary people.

Prayer Calendar from the General Board of Global Ministries of The United Methodist Church. Using this yearly calendar daily will encourage you to pray for missionaries on their birthdays and will remind you of the many ways United Methodists are responding to the needs of people around the globe. To order, call the Service Center at 800-305-9857 and ask for Stock Number 2818.

Responsible Grace: John Wesley's Practical Theology, by Randy L. Maddox (Nashville: Abingdon Press, 1994).

The United Methodist Reporter. Read this publication to discover ways United Methodists are living their faith. Address: UMR Communications, P.O. Box 660275, Dallas, TX 75266-0275. Phone: 800-947-0207. Internet: http://www.umr.org

Teacher Development Workshop:
Mission and Ministry in the World

Purpose
The purpose of this workshop is to help teachers and small-group leaders explore the need to connect works of piety with works of mercy.

Scripture
Matthew 28:18-20; Acts 2:8; Mark 1:16-20; 1 Corinthians 12:4-7; Luke 2:8-18 and 4:16-21; John 4:7-29; Acts 8:1-8

Time
This session is designed to last two hours.

Materials
- Nametags
- Pencils
- Newsprint
- Felt-tip markers
- Masking tape
- Bibles
- Hymnals
- Photocopies (one per person) of the following:
  "Corner Conversations: Good News Witnesses" (page 50)
  "Acts of Piety/Acts of Mercy Self-Assessment" (page 51)
  "Gifts Unwrapped" (page 52)
  "Tuesday's Child" (page 53)

Preparation
- Review the workshop plan and adapt it, as necessary, to your congregation.
- Write the purpose statement of this workshop on newsprint.
- Photocopy the handouts (pages 50–53).
- Gather the supplies listed above.
- Display signs numbering the four corners of the room.

Workshop Outline
- Gathering and Group Building (10 minutes)
- Remember Invitations to Follow Jesus (40 minutes)
- Bible Study and Reflection (40 minutes)
- Self-Assessment of Piety/Mercy (10 Minutes)
- Making Use of the Spirit's Gifts (10 minutes)
- Closing (10 minutes)

Workshop Plan

Gathering and Group Building (10 minutes)

❶ Welcome participants and ask them to make nametags, if necessary. Then ask participants to find a partner and tell him or her how they spent last Sunday's hours.

❷ Ask participants to find a new partner and tell him or her how they spent last Tuesday's hours.

❸ Call the participants together. Lead the group in a prayer, using your own words or the following: "Holy God, giver of all our moments and days, we give you thanks for this group of ordinary people who have chosen to invest a portion of this day so that we may strengthen our skills as teachers and leaders. We thank you for your presence here with us and ask you to guide our minds and hearts as we work together. Amen."

❹ On newsprint write the following words: *Jerusalem, Judea, Samaria, ends of the earth.*

❺ Let volunteers read aloud Matthew 28:18-20 and Acts 2:8. Then ask the group to sing the first and second stanzas of "We've a Story to Tell to the Nations" (*The United Methodist Hymnal,* 569).

Remember Invitations to Follow Jesus (40 minutes)

❶ Let a volunteer read aloud Mark 1:16-20. Then say: "Nudge your memory. Remember your earliest memory of feeling invited to follow Jesus. I'm not asking you to remember when you responded to the invitation to follow. I'm asking when you first felt invited. Think a moment, keeping your memories to yourself. How old were you? Now, nudge your neighbor and tell your story."

❷ When conversations begin to wane, say: "You have just participated in evangelism. God has touched your life, and you have witnessed to that good news."

❸ Ask how many people remembered something that happened before the age of three. Let volunteers tell their stories to the total group. Ask who remembered something that happened between the ages of three and five. Let volunteers tell their stories. Repeat the process twice more, letting volunteers who remembered an event between the ages of six and nine tell their stories, and volunteers who remembered an event that occurred after the age of nine tell their stories.

❹ Say: "Invitations to follow Jesus come to people of all ages. Invitations come in different ways. We are here today because we have been invited to follow Jesus. Ages differed, experiences differed, but someone somewhere made us feel that we were invited to follow Jesus. God was present at all those invitational events—working through witnesses."

Bible Study and Reflection (40 minutes)

❶ Distribute photocopies of "Corner Conversations: Good News Witnesses" (page 50). Ask participants to divide into groups by moving to the numbered corners of the room. Explain that their group's Scripture passage on the handout corresponds with the number in their corner. Allow each group to spend about twenty minutes reading and studying the Scripture, following the instructions on the handout.

❷ Let each small group report the highlights of their discussion to the total group. Say: "We are evangelists. We share God's good news in Jerusalem (within the walls of our church building). We witness in Judea (in our neighborhoods, at our jobs, in our daily activities). As part of a connectional church, we have opportunities to witness to the ends of the earth."

Self-Assessment of Piety/Mercy (10 Minutes)

❶ Read aloud the first two paragraphs from "For the Leader" (page 45).

❷ Distribute photocopies of "Acts of Piety/Acts of Mercy Self Assessment" (page 51) and ask participants to complete the assessment.

Making Use of the Spirit's Gifts (10 Minutes)

❶ Let a volunteer read aloud 1 Corinthians 12:4-7.

❷ Say: "Gifts are intended to be unwrapped, put to use, enjoyed. God has gifted each of us with special abilities. Those abilities are to be unwrapped and used for our Sunday-type days and for our Tuesday-type days. In all our days, in all our ways, rooted firmly in the grace of God, we are to love God and neighbor."

❸ Distribute photocopies of "Gifts Unwrapped" (page 52) and ask participants to complete and sign the agreement.

Closing (10 minutes)

❶ Ask participants to remember the first two lines of the nursery rhyme "Monday's Child" (Monday's child is fair of face, Tuesday's child is full of grace).

❷ Say: "Perhaps the metaphor of Tuesday's child can help us. As teachers and small-group leaders, we usually recognize our usefulness within the walls of Jerusalem (the institutional church). But, filled with God's grace, we are called to serve faithfully in Judea (beyond the walls of the institutional church). Our Tuesday-type days are filled with opportunities to love God and neighbor."

❸ Distribute photocopies of "Tuesday's Child" (page 53) and lead the group in singing the song as a closing prayer. Or let volunteers read the stanzas of this song aloud. Then lead the group in singing "Here I Am, Lord" (*The United Methodist Hymnal*, 593) for your closing prayer.

Good News Witnesses

Evangelist—from a Greek word meaning "messenger of good tidings." In the early church, evangelists were distinct from apostles, prophets, pastors, and teachers (Ephesians 4:11). Later, the name *evangelist* was given to the writers of the four Gospels.

Gospel—from an Anglo-Saxon word meaning "good news" or "good story." For Christians, the good news is of Jesus Christ, the kingdom of God, and salvation.

Group 1—Luke 2:8-18

Group 2—Luke 4:16-21

Group 3—John 4:7-29

Group 4—Acts 8:1-8

Read the Scripture passage assigned to your group; then discuss the following questions as they relate to your assigned reading:

❶ Who was the evangelist(s)?

❷ What was the good-news message?

❸ To whom was the good-news message addressed?

❹ In what ways does this Scripture passage give you comfort?

❺ In what ways does this Scripture passage make you uncomfortable?

Acts of Piety/Acts of Mercy

Read each statement; then use a 1 through 5 designation to rate your current practice (1=rarely; 5=consistently).

Acts of Piety

___ Bible reading/study is a part of my day.

___ Prayer is a part of my day.

___ I take time to be quiet and focused on God.

___ I experience God's presence in my life.

___ I am filled with a sense of thanksgiving.

___ My life has meaning and purpose.

___ I seek opportunities for spiritual growth.

___ I participate in weekly worship services.

Acts of Mercy

___ My faith shapes my daily decisions.

___ My faith shapes my daily actions.

___ I share my personal resources with others.

___ I embrace equality for all.

___ I work to protect the environment.

___ I seek out opportunities to help others.

___ I want to reduce pain and suffering in the world.

___ I believe that the church should be an agent of social change.

Unwrapped

Grace—an unearned gift from God

_____

Whereas, I have witnessed the following situation in need of God's good news:

and whereas God, the party of the first part, has graced me with the following abilities:

❶

❷

❸

I, the party of the second part, agree to use my God-gifted abilities to address this situation in these specific ways:

❶

❷

❸

_____   _____

(signed)   (date)

Tuesday's Child

WORDS AND MUSIC: Joyce Brown.

With Teaching

FOR THE **LEADER**

How can I teach to make a difference? How can I make the Bible exciting? How can I hold their interest? How do children, youth, and adults learn? These are some of the questions asked by teachers and those responsible for Christian education in churches. All are good questions. We can provide guidelines, knowing full well that each church, each class, and each person is different.

First things first. You teach in everything you do. Sometimes this occurs in a formal classroom setting. Sometimes Christian education occurs when you put the curriculum aside and deal with a class member who is hurting, or when you model Jesus' love as you deal with the children's behavior, or when you stop what you are doing to pray about something that has happened in your world (a new baby or a fire in the community).

Sometimes Christian education is you. Students and members of small groups see teachers and church leaders as role models. They believe that what you say or do is right. For weeks we assumed our son's first-grade teacher's name was "Mrs. Chaccini Says." And whatever Mrs. Chaccini said was the right answer. As a teacher, you have awesome power to shape lives.

The following are three of the top qualities of a "good" Sunday school teacher or small-group leader: loves and cares for students, has a faith to share, understands how people grow and learn.

Think about it. The ultimate lesson you are teaching is to love God and love neighbor. When you love your students, tell stories about your personal relationship with God, and present material in interesting and age-appropriate ways, you accomplish what Christian education is all about. Please note that all of these qualities begin with verbs. You, as teachers and leaders, must take action. You have to be active participants in the teaching/learning process.

by Barbara Bruce

Section 5

If God has called you to teach, celebrate by viewing teaching and learning as a way of growing in biblical knowledge and faith.

When you take time to know your students, their interests, their particular learning needs, what makes them laugh, and what excites them, you are saying you love them. When you tell your stories of the role of God in your life, faith is caught rather than taught.

I love to use a twist on an old cliché: "Those who can, teach. Those who can't, find some less-significant form of work." God has gifted you to teach. God has called you into this most important ministry of changing and shaping lives.

You, as teachers, must put something of yourselves into the lesson. Otherwise, you are being mechanical and distanced. When you take the words off the sheets of curriculum and make them yours, you please God, your students, and yourself. You can make the lesson your own in one hundred ways. Giving a lesson your personal touch usually cannot happen if you look at your lesson over Sunday morning coffee or in the car on the way to church. You need to read the Scripture and discover what it is saying to you. Live with the Scripture for the week and listen for God's still, small voice. Gather the materials you need, or use the ideas in curriculum in a unique and personal way. Don't say yes to this ministry unless you can give the gift of yourself to teaching and to God.

Most people will agree that the best way to learn something is to teach it. You seldom fail to learn as you prepare to teach. Much insightful learning about the Bible and its lessons for life come as you plan and prepare for a class. God often calls you to teach what you need to learn.

Listening to your students and tuning in to their questions may provide insight and new ways of viewing Scripture. Being an active participant in the learning helps you to stretch and grow. Remember, it is better to say "I don't know" to a question than to try to fake it. People of all ages will respect your honesty and disrespect your deception. Take a question and turn it into a teachable moment by making the discoveries together.

Teaching is a soul-making thing to do! If God has called you to teach, celebrate by viewing teaching and learning as a way of growing in biblical knowledge and faith. Pray about God's message you are imparting. Pray about touching and transforming lives. Pray for your students. Ask your students to pray for you. Open your heart and mind as you invite God to guide you as you grow in this awesome ministry.

Helpful Resources

Frames of Mind: The Theory of Multiple Intelligences, by Howard Gardner (New York: Basic Books, 1993).

Harvard Project Zero Web site (http://pzweb.harvard.edu). Project Zero's mission is to understand and enhance learning, thinking, and creativity in the arts, as well as humanistic and scientific disciplines.

Multiple Intelligences: The Complete MI Book, by Spencer Kagan and Miguel Kagan (San Clemente, CA: Kagan Cooperative Learning, 1998).

New Horizons for Learning Web site (http://www.newhorizons.org). This Web site has information on emerging trends and strategies in teaching and learning.

7 Ways of Teaching the Bible to Children, by Barbara Bruce (Nashville: Abingdon Press, 1996).

Teacher Development Workshop:
Teaching and Learning

Purpose

The purpose of this workshop is to help teachers and small-group leaders explore ways to teach creatively, based on the variety of ways people learn.

Scripture

Psalm 126:1-3

Time

This session is designed to last approximately two to three hours.

Materials

- Bibles
- Newsprint
- Felt-tip markers
- Masking tape
- Pencils
- Peanuts in the shell (one per person)
- Photocopies (one per person) of the following:
  "10½ Ways of Teaching Creatively" (page 61)
  "Learning With Our Whole Being" (page 62)
  "Different Ways of Learning" (page 63)
  "Knowing Your Students" (page 64)

Preparation

- Review the workshop plan and adapt it, as necessary, to your congregation.
- Write the purpose statement of this workshop on newsprint.
- Photocopy the handouts (pages 61–64).
- Gather the supplies listed above.

Workshop Outline

- Gathering and Group Building (20–30 minutes)
- Explore Ways to Teach Creatively (45–60 minutes)
- Explore Different Ways of Learning (20–30 minutes)
- Plan to Use Different Learning Preferences (50–60 minutes)
- Closing (5–10 minutes)

Workshop Plan

Gathering and Group Building (20–30 minutes)

❶ After everyone has arrived, introduce yourself and state the purpose of the workshop. Ask the participants to introduce themselves and answer these questions: Why are you here today? What do you expect to gain from this time together? Record the participants' expectations on newsprint.

❷ Read aloud Psalm 126:1-3. Ask the participants to recall other Scripture passages that mention joy and laughter. Then say: "Sometimes we take ourselves too seriously and miss the joy and fulfillment that comes from teaching God's Word."

❸ Ask the participants to form groups of three and discuss briefly where they experience joy in teaching and when they take themselves too seriously in teaching. Invite volunteers to tell the entire group the highlights of their conversations.

Explore Ways to Teach Creatively (45–60 minutes)

❶ Give each participant a photocopy of "10 ½ Ways of Teaching Creatively" (page 61). Use the following suggestions to help participants think about these ideas.

- *Love your students.* Ask participants to close their eyes and picture a favorite Sunday school teacher. Now ask them to open their eyes and remember a specific lesson that teacher taught. Ask for insights and key learnings.

- *Share your faith.* Ask participants to think of one specific way they do or can share with their students their personal relationship with God. Invite volunteers to voice their thoughts.

- *Involve the whole person in the learning process.* Give each person a photo-copy of "Learning With Our Whole Being" (page 62). Ask participants to write on the handout some activities they could use in their current teaching situation that would encourage thinking (head). Do the same with hands, heart, and feet. Allow each person about five minutes to work individually. Then have them form groups of three (different from the groups they were in previously) and discuss their responses. Have them return to the total group; then ask for key learnings and insights.

- *Invite students into the learning process.* Ask participants to identify ways the idea of inviting students into the learning process has been modeled during the workshop. Ask for additional suggestions for involving the students in the learning process. Record the suggestions on newsprint.

- *Practice praise and affirmation.* Ask participants how they feel when they are praised. Then ask how they feel when they are ignored. Have them discuss with one other person how these practices affect teaching and learning.

- *Encourage lots of right answers.* Ask participants to think of a question from a recent lesson they have taught that has many "right" answers. (Example: How, do you think, was the boy with the five barley loaves and two fish in John 6:9 affected by his experience?) After giving the participants a few minutes to think, ask for volunteers to give examples. Discuss the difference between questions that encourage thinking and those that limit answers. Explain that both kinds of questions are important. Questions with one right answer are informational questions. (How many barley loaves did the boy have?) Questions that may have many right answers are formational questions. To inspire students to think creatively and to become involved with the story or topic, we need to ask more formational questions.

- *Ask "what if" and "why" questions.* Explain that asking these types of questions is another way of asking formational questions. (What if the boy had tried to sell his loaves and fish to Jesus?) "What if" and "why" questions stimulate thinking and help students encounter the story. Invite participants to give examples of "what if" and "why" questions they could have used in a recent teaching situation.

- *Laugh.* Have the participants name ways that laughter facilitates learning. Remind them that while humor can be an extremely powerful tool in teaching and learning, humor that is used to ridicule can be equally destructive. Ask the participants to discuss briefly with one or two other people what teaching with love and laughter might look like in their teaching situation.

- *Use mistakes as learning opportunities.* Encourage participants to think about how students' wrong answers or misinformation might be used as a teaching tool without making the students feel dumb. Ask for volunteers to remember examples from their own experience.

- *Use methods and activities that stimulate different ways of learning.* Explain that later in this workshop they will be focusing in more depth on the different ways that people learn.

❷ Encourage the participants to post the "10 ½ Ways of Teaching Creatively" handout on their refrigerator or somewhere else where they will see it frequently.

Explore Different Ways of Learning (20–30 minutes)

❶ Give each participant a peanut (still in the shell) and tell them to "get to know their peanut." After about forty-five seconds, collect all the peanuts and spread them on the floor. Have the participants find their peanuts. Ask them to reflect on how they found their own peanut and how this activity is like teaching. Then say: "If all those we teach are unique individuals, why do we sometimes teach as if they are all the same?" Allow a few moments for silent reflection.

❷ Give each person a photocopy of "Different Ways of Learning" (page 63) and review together the information on the handout. Then hand out photocopies of "Knowing Your Students" (page 64). Ask the participants to list the members of their class or group down one side of the page. Review again the various learning preferences. As you review each preference, ask participants to place a check mark beside the members' names whom they believe prefer to learn in that specific way.

Plan to Use Different Learning Preferences (50–60 minutes)

❶ Divide the group into eight smaller groups. (If you have a small group, you may need to have fewer groups.) Assign each group one of the learning preferences discussed in the previous activity and a Scripture passage. (You may want to use Scripture passages from upcoming lessons.) If you have fewer than eight groups, assign more than one learning preference to each group. Ask the groups to plan a learning experience based on the Scripture they have been given and using the learning preference they have been assigned.

❷ Bring the group back together after about fifteen minutes, and let each small group describe the learning experience they have planned. If you are doing this in a longer retreat-type setting, allow each group to actually lead the experience they have planned.

❸ After each group has reported back, use the following questions as a springboard for further discussion:
- What insights did you gain from this experience?
- When you teach, which learning preferences do you incorporate most often?
- What ideas do you have for ways of incorporating other learning preferences?
- What are some learning activities that involve several learning preferences.

Closing (5–10 minutes)

❶ Ask each participant to think of one new thing they are going to try, based on today's workshop. Allow volunteers to tell the rest of the group what they will do.

❷ Close with a prayer asking God to grant these leaders patience, humor, insight, and creativity as they teach.

10½ Ways of

Teaching Creatively

1. Love your students.
2. Share your faith.
3. Involve the whole person in the learning process.
4. Invite students into the learning process.
5. Practice praise and affirmation.
6. Encourage lots of right answers.
7. Ask "what if" and "why" questions.
8. Laugh.
9. Use mistakes as learning opportunities.
10. Use methods and activities that stimulate different ways of learning.
10½. See Number 1.

Our Whole Being

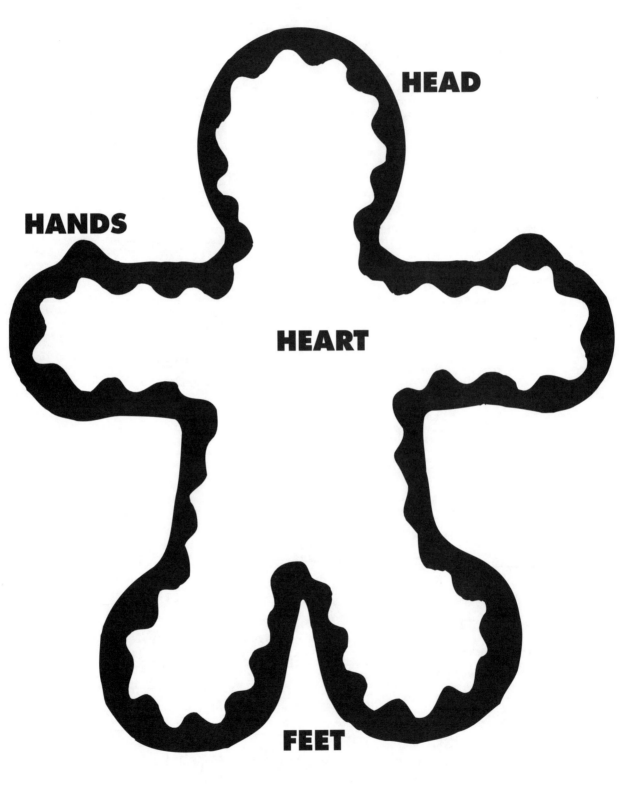

HEAD

HANDS

HEART

FEET

Different Ways **of Learning**

Dr. Howard Gardner of Harvard University founded an educational movement based on the theory that there are a variety of ways that people learn. This theory is called multiple intelligences (MI). Dr. Gardner has identified at least eight ways, and continuing research is likely to reveal even more. His research indicates that, while we are able to learn in a variety of ways, each individual has particular ways that are most effective and meaningful. As teachers and leaders of small groups, we can help others learn by creating settings in which they can use their preferred learning styles. The following chart gives basic information about each of the intelligences.

Type	Characteristics	Some Related Activities
Linguistic (Verbal)	• Able to relate words to symbols • Focuses on hearing and speaking abilities • Sensitive to word meanings, sounds, and order • Able to use language to influence, remember, explain, and reflect • Thinks in words	Poetry, storytelling, debate, spoken liturgy, discussion, creative writing, jokes/limericks
Musical (Rhythmic)	• Sensitive to melody, rhythm, tone, pitch, and timbre • Able to relate sounds to emotions and human character traits • Thinks in melody and lyrics	Singing, playing musical instruments, musical liturgy, composing, conducting
Logical-Mathematical	• Understands the concept of number, sequence, and numerical relationships • Able to see patterns of ideas • Able to put together chains of ideas • Understands cause and effect • Thinks in numbers and abstract symbols	Timelines, flow charts, cause-and-effect diagrams, logic problems, deciphering codes, cataloging
Spatial (Visual)	• Able to create a mental image and perform actions on the image • Sensitive to perspective, composition, and proportion • Thinks in pictures	Building models, painting, sculpture, visual aids, videos, guided imagery, designing
Bodily-Kinesthetic	• Control of body motions • Capable of handling objects skillfully • Thinks in movements, gestures, and body language	Mime, dance, sports, acting, construction, roleplaying, charades
Interpersonal	• Able to notice distinctions among other individuals, particularly related to their moods, motivations, and intentions • Makes and maintains friends easily	Group-building exercises, service projects, group problem-solving, cooperative learning projects
Intrapersonal	• Able to understand one's own feelings, strengths, and beliefs • Makes meaning by reflecting on experience	Journaling, theological reflection, silent reflection
Naturalist	• Able to sort and classify plants and animals • Aware of the natural world (animals, plants, minerals, and so forth)	Gardening, caring for pets, nature hikes, environmental-awareness activities

Knowing **Your Students**

Student's Name	Linguistic (Reading, writing, speaking)	Musical (Rhythms, singing, humming)	Logical-Mathematical (Problem-solving, sequencing, ordering)	Spatial (Visual) (Looking at charts and pictures, drawing)	Bodily-Kinesthetic (Manipulating objects, moving body)	Interpersonal (Interacting with others)	Intrapersonal (Reflecting, understanding one's self)	Naturalist (Connecting with the natural world)

Learning Preference

with God

FOR THE **LEADER**

The fundamental state of the Christian life is being in a relationship with God. On that relationship is founded all that takes place within us as well as what we live out in the world. If we are to receive the gift of the life abundant promised by God and be able to be loving servants of God—be the Church of Jesus Christ—then our relationship with God must become full and functional.

A relationship with God is nurtured through a way of living that includes time for God. Just as you would spend time with a friend in order to nurture that relationship, so it is necessary to spend time with God in order for that relationship to become all that it can be. This time with God has been called practicing the spiritual disciplines, which is a way we can receive God's grace.

No one list will describe the many ways that we can receive God's grace, but John Wesley mentioned the most basic ones in his General Rules, which are still part of *The Book of Discipline of The United Methodist Church*. Simply stated, we are to do no harm, to do good, and to attend to the ordinances of God. Wesley considered the ordinances of God to include public worship, Bible reading and study, the Lord's Supper, family and private prayer, Christian conversation or conferencing, and fasting or abstinence.

All of these activities are ways that we put ourselves in a position to receive God's love. In one sense, we can say that all of these are a form of prayer, of being intentionally aware of and focusing on God's presence with us and wanting to nurture that relationship, of "resting in God." We could say that all of the Christian life is resting in God and that the fruit of that relationship is our loving lives.

There are some basic orientations of our perspective that give greater depth and meaning to our practice of the disciplines. The first is our intentionality. Do we make a definite, regular effort to spend time with God in the same way

Adapted from material written by Ben Marshall

Section 6

we make it a definite point to spend time with our friends? This is not necessarily easy, because it is more difficult to sense the results of the time we spend in prayer. But if we want the relationship with God, we must spend that time; and when we do, we will experience tremendous results in our lives. We must simply be willing to wait for those results to make themselves known—and they will.

The second is the cultivation of openness to God's love. I must develop a willingness for God to love me, which means a willingness to feel that love within. This is not easy to explain, but it is a fundamental inner posture in our relationship with God. It is much like being willing for someone to give you an extravagant gift and simply being grateful and accepting without feeling you are not worthy of it. Openness is also a willingness to bring before God all of our deepest and darkest feelings so that they can experience the light of God's love and healing.

The third is the attention to all of the elements of a relationship with God. Those elements are our understanding or conceptual belief about God, our inner trust and assurance of God's love for us, and our loyalty to living out God's love in the world. We will need to work on all of these as we go through our lives, but we may need to pay more attention to some of them at certain times. For instance, if I have difficulty believing that God is unconditionally loving, then I may need to do some serious Bible study or theological discussion to help me come to know that as true for me. I may also need to learn more about prayer and practice it in order to grow in my trust in God's love.

Helpful Resources

Beginning Prayer, by John Killenger (Nashville: Upper Room Books, 1993).

Devotional Life in the Wesleyan Tradition, by Steve Harper (Nashville: Upper Room Books, 1999).

Grace Notes: Spirituality and the Choir, by Anne Burnette Hook (Nashville: Discipleship Resources, 1998).

Guide for Covenant Discipleship Groups, by Gayle Watson (Nashville: Discipleship Resources, 2000).

Living in the Presence: Spiritual Exercises to Open Our Lives to the Awareness of God, by Tilden Edwards (San Francisco: Harper SanFrancisco, 1995).

Open Mind, Open Heart: The Contemplative Dimension of the Gospel, by Thomas Keating (Rockport, MA: Element, 1992).

Seasons of Your Heart: Prayers and Reflections, by Macrina Wiederkehr (San Francisco: Harper SanFrancisco, 1991).

Soul Feast: An Invitation to the Christian Spiritual Life, by Marjorie J. Thompson (Louisville: Westminster John Knox Press, 1995).

The Song of the Seed: A Monastic Way of Tending the Soul, by Macrina Wiederkehr (San Francisco: Harper SanFrancisco, 1997).

Just as you would spend time with a friend in order to nurture that relationship, so it is necessary to spend time with God in order for that relationship to become all that it can be.

Teacher Development Workshop:
Practicing the Spiritual Disciplines

Purpose
The purpose of this series of workshops is to help teachers and small-group leaders grow in their relationship to God by exploring and experiencing spiritual disciplines.

Scripture
Genesis 12:1-5; Psalm 62:1; 1 John 4:9-10

Time
This section is designed for six sessions that last approximately one to one and a half hours each. It can be done over a series of weeks or as a two-day retreat. If you are doing it in a retreat-type setting, allow time between sessions for participants to practice and process what has been presented.

Materials
FOR ALL SESSIONS
- Bibles
- Hymnals
- Pencils
- Paper
- ■ Newsprint
- Felt-tip markers
- Masking tape

SESSION 1
- Photocopies (one per person) of "Personal Prayer" (page 75)

SESSION 2
- Photocopies (one per person) of "My Spiritual History" (page 76) and "Praying the Scriptures" (page 77)

SESSION 4
- Photocopies (one per person) of "Active Worship" (page 78)

SESSION 6
- *The United Methodist Book of Worship*

Preparation
- Arrange for space that is conducive to small-group discussion.
- If you are doing this in a retreat-type setting, arrange for housing, food, and transportation.
- Review the workshop plan and adapt it, as necessary, to your congregation.
- Write the purpose statement of this workshop on newsprint.
- Photocopy the handouts (pages 75–78).
- Gather the supplies listed above.

Workshop Outline

SESSION 1: The Spiritual Discipline of Prayer
Gathering and Group Building (15–20 minutes)
Explore the Scripture (20–30 minutes)
Focus on Prayer (15–20 minutes)
Closing (5 minutes)

SESSION 2: The Spiritual Discipline of Scripture Study
Gathering and Group Building (5–10 minutes)
Spiritual Histories (50–70 minutes)
Using the Scriptures to Pray (15–20 minutes)
Closing (5–10 minutes)

SESSION 3: The Spiritual Discipline of Acts of Mercy
Gathering and Group Building (10–15 minutes)
Prayer as Receptivity (10–15 minutes)
Acts of Mercy as a Spiritual Discipline (30–40 minutes)
Closing (5 minutes)

SESSION 4: The Spiritual Discipline of Public Worship
Gathering and Group Building (10–15 minutes)
Experience Journaling Prayer (25–35 minutes)
Public Worship as a Spiritual Discipline (10–20 minutes)
Closing (5 minutes)

SESSION 5: The Spiritual Discipline of Letting Go
Gathering and Group Building (10–15 minutes)
Prayer as Movement (15–25 minutes)
Letting Go as a Spiritual Discipline (20–30 minutes)
Closing (5 minutes)

SESSION 6: The Spiritual Discipline of Holy Communion
Gathering and Group Building (10–15 minutes)
Holy Communion as a Spiritual Discipline (15–20 minutes)
Closing (30–40 minutes)

Workshop Plan

Session 1: The Spiritual Discipline of Prayer

Gathering and Group Building (15–20 minutes)

❶ After everyone has arrived, ask participants to introduce themselves by telling their names and describing their earliest memory of anything related to God.

❷ Explain that this series of sessions is designed to help members of the group grow in their relationship with God. It will do this by focusing on prayer and other spiritual disciplines. In each session, participants will experience a different form of prayer and will explore a particular spiritual discipline. If you are doing this in a retreat-type setting, review the schedule and other housekeeping details.

❸ Help the group set ground rules for participation, such as the following:
  ☐ Listen to one another first and respond later.
  ☐ Confidentiality will be maintained by all group members.
  ☐ Each person's spiritual journey is valid and holy.
  ☐ In any group discussions, it is acceptable for a member to say "pass" if he or she does not want to say anything.

Explore the Scripture (20–30 minutes)

❶ Read aloud Genesis 12:1-5. Divide the group into smaller groups of two to three and ask them to discuss the following questions in light of the Scripture they have just heard:
  ☐ What, do you think, does it mean to be called on a journey by God?
  ☐ If we think of this story in terms of a spiritual journey, rather than a physical one, what does it mean to leave your country and family and go to a new place?
  ☐ What, do you think, does it mean to be blessed to be a blessing?
  ☐ Where are you on your spiritual journey?

❷ Gather the group together and let volunteers report insights from their discussion.

Focus on Prayer (15–20 minutes)

❶ Remind the group that prayer is a primary way we grow in our relationship with God. In fact, one way to define *prayer* is "anything we do, think, or feel that puts us in touch with God." Invite participants to talk with one another about their prayer life—not what happens in it, but what kinds of things they do as a part of their prayer time (reading, meditating, talking with God). Assure the group that there is not one right way to pray and that each individual's journey will be honored in the group.

❷ Give each person a photocopy of "Personal Prayer" (page 75). Encourage them to try some of the suggestions during the individual time during the retreat or before the next session if you are meeting over a series of weeks.

❸ Have a time of prayer. Invite volunteers to make prayer requests. Have a time of silent prayer. Then close with a prayer specifically mentioning the prayer requests that have been made.

❹ Ask each member to pray for all the other group members each day.

Closing (5 minutes)

Close with a brief prayer, or simply say: "May God's peace go with us."

Session 2: The Spiritual Discipline of Scripture Study

Gathering and Group Building (5–10 minutes)

❶ If you are doing this over a series of weeks, allow time for participants to reflect on how their prayer life has gone since the last meeting and what it has meant to know that others are praying for them.

❷ Begin the session with a hymn or song.

Spiritual Histories (50–70 minutes)

❶ Give each person a photocopy of "My Spiritual History" (page 76) and ask them to follow the directions on the page. Explain that when they have finished working individually, they will be explaining their chart to the rest of the group. Have newsprint and felt-tip markers available for those who choose to do their chart in a larger format.

❷ Gather the group back together and let each person describe his or her chart to the entire group.

❸ After everyone has had an opportunity to speak, ask the group to reflect on insights they gained from doing this exercise.

❹ Suggest that the group members begin doing a mini-spiritual history of each day during their prayer time. This is simply taking a few minutes in God's presence and thinking back over the day, identifying those times when you seemed the farthest from God and times when you seemed closest, when you felt joy and peace, and when you felt alone or angry or anxious.

Using the Scriptures to Pray (15–20 minutes)

❶ Remind the group that Wesley considered study of the Scriptures to be a spiritual discipline. Although there are many ways of studying the Scriptures, one way that has been helpful to many people is called *lectico divina* ("divine reading"), which is a way of reading the Scriptures that involves both our hearts and heads.

❷ Give each person a photocopy of "Praying the Scriptures" (page 77) and explain that this is one model of devotional reading of the Bible. Review the steps outlined on the handout.

❸ Ask the group members to try this way of praying before the next session. If you are doing this in a retreat-type setting, make sure to schedule enough individual time before the next session to allow for this.

Closing (5–10 minutes)

Close by inviting each person to do a sentence prayer.

Session 3: The Spiritual Discipline of Acts of Mercy

Gathering and Group Building (10–15 minutes)

❶ Begin with a hymn or song.

❷ Invite volunteers to tell the group anything they would like that is related to their experience with praying the Scriptures or with doing daily spiritual histories.

Prayer as Receptivity (10–15 minutes)

❶ Read aloud Psalm 62:1 and 1 John 4:9-10. Point out that both of these passages focus on God's action, rather than ours. Psalm 62:1 speaks of our role in waiting in silence for God; 1 John 4:9-10 reminds us of God's love for us. While in prayer, we are sometimes actively talking to God; sometimes we are receiving God's love.

❷ Ask the participants to sit quietly with their eyes closed, breathing slowly and steadily. After allowing them to sit silently for a short time, say in a slow, quiet voice: "As you breathe in, receive God's love into your life. Feel God's love flowing throughout your body, giving you confidence and peace. As you breath out, let go of those things that are hindering your ability to receive God's love. Breathe out the fear, anxiety, and anger. Continue to breathe in and out. With each inhaling breath, receive God's love. With each exhaling breath, breathe out those things that inhibit you from receiving God's love. Use whatever mental images are helpful as you do this." Continue in silence for a few more minutes; then quietly say: "Amen."

Acts of Mercy as a Spiritual Discipline (30–40 minutes)

❶ Remind the group that "doing good" is part of John Wesley's General Rules. Wesley understood that good works could be a means of grace. We do not do good works to earn God's love, but rather as a way of experiencing God's love. How we go about doing acts of love and mercy depends on the gifts and talents God has given us. There are many needs for our love in this world, and it is our calling to respond to them with all that we are, but uniquely as we are.

❷ Ask the group members to write down three gifts (skills, talents, abilities, interests) that God has given them. Then ask them to spend some time in silent prayer, considering how God might be calling them to use these gifts to help others.

❸ Divide the group into pairs to discuss where they feel God is calling them. Encourage each person to commit to doing at least one thing in the next week, based on the urgings they are feeling from God.

Closing (5 minutes)

Close with a prayer thanking God for the gifts of the group and asking for guidance in using those gifts faithfully.

Session 4: The Spiritual Discipline of Public Worship

Gathering and Group Building (10–15 minutes)

❶ Begin with a hymn or song.

❷ If you are doing this over a series of weeks, allow time for participants to reflect on how their prayer life has gone since the last meeting and how they have experienced acts of mercy as a means of grace.

Experience Journaling Prayer (25–35 minutes)

❶ Explain that for many people, keeping a journal can be a meaningful way of praying. Spiritual journaling is different from keeping a diary. Rather, it is a way of using the written word to have a conversation with God that can facilitate inner clarity and expression.

❷ Give each participant a sheet of paper and pencil, and ask them to spend about twenty minutes in a written conversation with God. Let them know that they will not be asked to reveal what they have written.

❸ After the twenty minutes have passed, call the group back together. Ask for people's reactions to this form of prayer. Ask: "Was it more or less difficult than you had expected? Was there anything that surprised you about the experience? Would you want to incorporate this into your regular prayer time?"

Public Worship as a Spiritual Discipline (10–20 minutes)

❶ Explain that public (or corporate) worship is not just something we watch on Sunday morning but is an active way that we can experience God's grace. Ask for volunteers to tell what parts of corporate worship are most sacred for them.

❷ Hand out photocopies of "Active Worship" (page 78) and review the suggestions on the sheet. Use these as a springboard to further discussion about making corporate worship a spiritual discipline.

Closing (5 minutes)

Close with a time of silence or spontaneous spoken prayers from the group.

Session 5: The Spiritual Discipline of Letting Go

Gathering and Group Building (10–15 minutes)

1 Begin with a hymn or song.

2 If you are doing this over a series of weeks, allow time for participants to reflect on how their prayer life has gone since the last meeting. If some members of the group have begun to practice journaling, they may want to report how they have incorporated it into their lives.

Prayer as Movement (15–25 minutes)

1 Say: "When we think of prayer, words such as *silence*, *quiet*, and *still* come to mind. However, prayer can also be physically active. Singing, dancing, and moving are just a few of the forms of active prayer."

2 Divide the group into groups of two or three. Ask each group to choose a favorite hymn or prayer (or to make up their own) and to create simple movements to go with it.

3 When the small groups are finished, let each group teach their movements to the rest of the group.

Letting Go as a Spiritual Discipline (20–30 minutes)

1 Say: "John Wesley mentions fasting and abstinence in his list of spiritual disciplines. Many people today misunderstand what these mean. It seems most helpful to look at fasting and abstinence in a broad way as letting go of those things in our lives that have become more important than is healthy or helpful to us. Abstaining for a time from something you like is a symbol of how much more important God is to you than that particular thing. This can be a helpful way of growing in relationship with God. If we make things more important than God, our lives will become unhealthy.

"The form of letting go that is most appropriate for you is based on an examination of your own life to discover an unhealthy attachment to something. Or the letting go may be symbolic: choosing something that is not necessarily unhealthy, but that can be too important to you. The letting go in either case is a meaningful symbol of the importance of your relationship with God."

2 Ask if any members of the group have had the experience of giving up something as a spiritual discipline. Some members of the group may have had such an experience during Lent. Let volunteers tell what was meaningful and what was difficult about the experience.

3 Divide the group into pairs and ask each pair to discuss attachments that they have that would be helpful to give up. Suggest that they may want to encourage each other in their letting go by checking with each other on a regular basis.

Closing (5 minutes)

Close with one of the motion prayers the group developed earlier in the session.

Session 6: The Spiritual Discipline of Holy Communion

Gathering and Group Building (10–15 minutes)

❶ Begin with one of the motion prayers that the group developed in the previous session.

❷ If you are doing this over a series of weeks, allow time for participants to reflect on how their prayer life has gone since the last meeting. If members of the group have practiced the spiritual discipline of letting go, encourage them to report on how their spiritual lives have been affected by this practice.

Holy Communion as a Spiritual Discipline (15–20 minutes)

❶ Say: "The sacrament of the Lord's Supper is a central act of our growing in God's love. It is an outward sign of an inward grace. The outward sign—going to the table or chancel rail, kneeling, receiving, and eating and drinking—is simply a symbol of something that God is seeking to have happen in us inwardly, spiritually. As the bread and juice nourish us physically, so God's love nourishes us spiritually. We are honored guests at God's table, and we are not alone at that table."

❷ Ask participants to discuss what they find most meaningful about Holy Communion. Suggest the following:

- As you go to the chancel rail, look around you at those going with you. Acknowledge your relationship with them. Remember that you are not alone and that you are loved in your community.
- Hear the words of consecration as a statement of how much God loves us.
- When you are being served, hold your hands together, with palms up to receive the bread, not taking it but letting the server place it in your hands as an expression of your willingness to receive from God.
- When you take the bread and juice, imagine it as your taking into your life God's love for you; and just as the taste of the bread and juice affect your body, so let God's love enliven your life.
- Be sure to give thanks in your heart for the free gift given to you by God, who is present and serving you with love.

Closing (30–40 minutes)

❶ Help the group remember what they have done over the course of these six sessions. Discuss what experiences they found most meaningful and how the sessions could have been improved.

❷ Some participants may want to continue to meet on a regular basis to learn more about the spiritual disciplines and support one another in their spiritual growth. You may need to set up another time with them to help them organize. One form of an ongoing group would be a Covenant Discipleship group. See "Helpful Resources" (page 66) for resources related to Covenant Discipleship.

❸ If there is a clergy person in the group, have him or her lead the group in a service of Holy Communion. If you do not have a clergy person, you can have a love feast. See pages 581–84 in *The United Methodist Book of Worship* for an order of worship for the love feast.

Prayer is not just sitting quietly, with hands folded, and reciting to God a list of what we want. Prayer is a way of listening to and speaking with God. Prayer can involve our voices, our thoughts, our actions. Prayer can take many different forms. Below you will find several suggestions for prayer. As you try different forms of prayer, some will undoubtedly be more meaningful to you than others. That's all right. There is not one right way to pray, and each individual must discover through experience his or her own way.

Conversation

This is the form of prayer that you are probably most familiar with. It is simply talking with God. Some people find it helpful to talk out loud, while others talk to God silently.

Journaling

This is talking with God on paper. It is a form of conversation that can facilitate inner clarity and expression.

Reflection

This is also referred to as meditation and often is characterized by reading Scripture or other devotional material, a time of silence, and a time of applying what we know to be God's promises to our life situation.

Imagery

This is using mental images to visualize ourselves in a relationship with God in a way that helps us deepen that relationship.

Body Posture and Movements

This may be used with other forms of prayer. It can include kneeling, dancing, walking, and other movements.

Silence

This is also called contemplation and is a way in which we allow our thoughts to become quiet and simply exist in God's presence, trusting that God's love is coming to us as we are silent.

History

My Spiritual

Think back on your life and remember those points that have had significant spiritual significance for you. These might include your first memories of feeling loved and accepted, times when you experienced God in new ways, events that had spiritual significance for you, and so forth. Your spiritual history may also include low points.

Some people will find it helpful to use the timeline below to chart their spiritual history; others will find it more helpful to draw symbols or write in prose. Use whatever method you prefer to record your spiritual history.

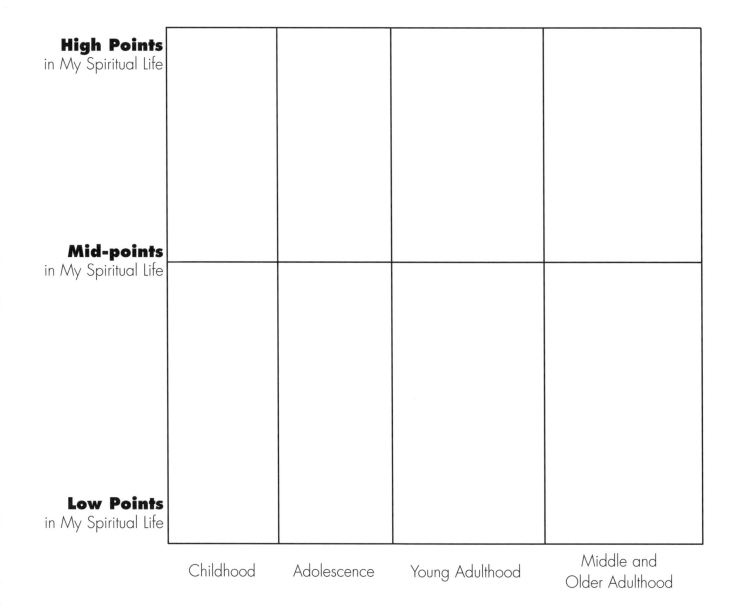

High Points
in My Spiritual Life

Mid-points
in My Spiritual Life

Low Points
in My Spiritual Life

| Childhood | Adolescence | Young Adulthood | Middle and Older Adulthood |

Praying the

Scriptures

Lectico divina ("divine reading") is a method of reading the Bible that has been a part of Christian tradition for hundreds of years. It is a method that involves our heads and our hearts. Outlined below is one method of divine reading. Try incorporating it into your life of prayer and study.

Step One: Read the Scripture

Begin with an attitude of quiet anticipation, remembering that you are in the presence of God. Pick a passage of Scripture to read; then read it without trying to focus on its meaning. Use your imagination to experience the setting of the passage. Imagine what you would see, smell, hear, feel, and taste if you were present in the passage.

Step Two: Meditate on the Scripture

Read the passage again, thinking about what the passage would have meant to the people who first heard it. Imagine yourself as each character in the passage and think about its meaning to them.

Step Three: Pray

Read the passage again, thinking about your feelings related to the passage. Talk with God about feelings and issues the passage raises for you.

Step Four: Contemplate

Breath deeply and slowly, becoming relaxed and quiet. Allow your mind to go blank. As you sit quietly, notice any thoughts that form in your mind. This is a time to allow God to speak to you.

Worship

Active

Take an active stance in your worship. God is not somewhere else; God is right there in your heart and in the hearts of each person. Our calling is to pay attention to God and to be open to God's word in us and to us. In your worship let God be the audience, and show God how important God is to you.

1 When you enter worship, take a moment to be quiet and to acknowledge in your own mind and heart God's presence with you and with all who are in the congregation.

2 When you sing the hymns, sing them as words you are saying to God, who is actually present. Allow that sense of relationship to God to fill you as you sing.

3 When you listen to the anthem, let the words speak to God for you or be words that come from God to you, depending on how the anthem is directed.

4 During the pastoral prayer, you may simply want to be attentive to God, letting the words of the prayer flow through you to God.

5 As you pray the psalm or other congregational prayer, again let yourself say them inwardly to God, who is truly present.

6 When you give your offering, let it be that which you are truly giving to God.

Recognize that all hymns or anthems or other acts of worship may not truly enable your worship of God on a particular day. Our worship is imperfect corporately as well as privately, but God understands that. The importance lies in our being personally attentive to God during those times and letting God handle the rest.

Contributors

Krau
Carol F.
SECTION 1

Carol F. Krau is the Director of Teacher/Leader Development at the General Board of Discipleship of The United Methodist Church. Carol is a diaconal minister in the Tennessee Annual Conference and is the author of *Keeping in Touch: Christian Formation and Teaching.* Carol lives in Nashville, Tennessee.

Bunyi
Judith M.
SECTION 2

Judith M. Bunyi is the Director of Small Group Ministry at the General Board of Discipleship of The United Methodist Church. She is an ordained elder and member of the Iowa Annual Conference. She has a Ph.D. in speech communication, focusing on small-group communication. She has experience as both a leader and a participant in small groups in a variety of settings, including church, workplace, school, and community. Judith lives in Nashville, Tennessee.

Westfield
N. Lynne
SECTION 3

N. Lynne Westfield is a deacon in the Eastern Pennsylvania Conference of The United Methodist Church. She has a Ph.D. in religious education and is on the faculty of the Theological School of Drew University in Madison, New Jersey.

Brown
Joyce
SECTION 4

Joyce Brown writes children's curriculum for The United Methodist Church. As a Cokesbury curriculum consultant, she helps churches discover ways to choose and use curriculum resources for people of all ages. She teaches the Grades 4–5 Sunday school class and directs the elementary choir at Western Hills United Methodist Church in Fort Worth, Texas. Many of her volunteer hours are spent tutoring at the multicultural elementary school across the street from her church.

Bruce
Barbara
SECTION 5

Barbara Bruce is a Christian educator serving the Rush United Methodist Church near Rochester, New York. Barbara is author of *7 Ways of Teaching the Bible to Children, Teaching Children Bible Basics,* and numerous articles. Barbara provides training seminars for church leaders around the country. She gives hugs.

Marshall
Ben
SECTION 6

Ben Marshall is Minister for Adult Christian Formation at Lovers Lane United Methodist Church in Dallas, Texas. He is a long-time Christian educator who believes in and practices spiritual direction (along with his teaching) as a key element of ministry.